The New CETA: Effect on Public Service Employment Programs:

Final Report

WILLIAM MIRENGOFF

LESTER RINDLER

HARRY GREENSPAN

SCOTT SEABLOM

LOIS BLACK

COMMITTEE ON EVALUATION OF
EMPLOYMENT AND TRAINING PROGRAMS

Assembly of Behavioral and Social Sciences

National Research Council

D1064241

NATIONAL ACADEMY PRESS

Washington, D.C. 1980

The study reported in this book was supported by a grant from the Employment and Training Administration of the U.S. Department of Labor. Points of view or opinions stated in this document are those of the authors and do not necessarily represent the official positions of the U.S. Department of Labor.

Library of Congress Cataloging in Publication Data

Main entry under title:

The New CETA.

  Bibliography: p.
  1. Public service employment—United States—
Addresses, essays, lectures. 2. Manpower policy—
United States—Addresses, essays, lectures. I. Miren-
goff, William. II. National Research Council. Com-
mittee on Evaluation of Employment and Training Programs.
HD5713.6.U54N48   331.11'0973   80-18948
ISBN 0-309-03087-0

Available from

NATIONAL ACADEMY PRESS
2101 Constitution Avenue, N.W.
Washington, D.C. 20418
Printed in the United States of America

COMMITTEE ON EVALUATION OF EMPLOYMENT AND TRAINING PROGRAMS

REPORTS BY THE COMMITTEE ON EVALUATION OF EMPLOYMENT AND TRAINING PROGRAMS

The Comprehensive Employment and Training Act: Impact on People, Places, and Programs (1976)

Transition to Decentralized Manpower Programs: Eight Area Studies (1976)

The Comprehensive Employment and Training Act: Abstracts of Selected Studies (1976)

Employment and Training Programs: The Local View (1978)

CETA: Assessment and Recommendations (1978)

CETA: Manpower Programs Under Local Control (1978)

CETA: Assessment of Public Service Employment Programs (1980)

SURVEY AREAS AND FIELD RESEARCH ASSOCIATES

ARIZONA

Phoenix
Edward Heler, Assistant Professor, Center for Public Affairs, Arizona State University

Balance of Arizona
Constance M. LaMonica, formerly Special Assistant for Intergovernmental Relations, State of Arizona

CALIFORNIA

Long Beach
Pamela S. Tolbert, Research Associate, Institute for Social Science Research, University of California at Los Angeles

Orange County Consortium
Lynne G. Zucker, Assistant Professor, Department of Sociology, University of California at Los Angeles

San Joaquin Consortium
C. Daniel Vencill, Research Associate, Center for Applied Manpower Research

Stanislaus County
Linda Gruber, Research Associate, Center for Applied Manpower Research

FLORIDA

Pasco County
Pinellas County–St. Petersburg Consortium
Emil Bie, former Deputy Director, Office of Technical Support, U.S. Employment Service

ILLINOIS

Cook County

INDIANA

Gary
Douglas Windham, Associate Professor, Department of Education, University of Chicago

v

KANSAS

Kansas City–Wyandotte County Consortium
Anthony L. Redwood, Associate Professor, School of Business, University of Kansas

Topeka–Shawnee County Consortium
Charles E. Krider, Associate Professor, School of Business, University of Kansas

MAINE

Balance of Maine
Roderick A. Forsgren, Professor and Associate Dean, Graduate School, University of Maine

MICHIGAN

Calhoun County
E. Earl Wright, Director, W. E. Upjohn Institute for Employment Research

Lansing Tri-County Regional Manpower Consortium
Philip L. Scherer, Senior Research Economist, W. E. Upjohn Institute for Employment Research

MINNESOTA

St. Paul
Ramsey County
James E. Jernberg, Associate Director for Administration, School of Public Affairs, University of Minnesota

NEW JERSEY

Middlesex County
Union County
Jack Chernick, Professor, Institute of Management and Labor Relations, Rutgers University

NEW YORK

New York City
Lois Blume, Professor, New School for Social Research

NORTH CAROLINA

Raleigh Consortium
John E. S. Lawrence, Research Psychologist, Research Triangle Institute

Balance of North Carolina
Nancy Paulson, Planner, Research Triangle Institute

OHIO

Cleveland Area–Western Reserve Consortium
Grace Franklin, Research Associate, Mershon Center, Ohio State University

Lorain County
Mary K. Marvel, Assistant Professor, School of Public Administration, Ohio State University

PENNSYLVANIA

Chester County
Harry Greenspan, Research Associate, National Research Council

Philadelphia
Albert L. Shostack, former Chief, Division of Residential Living, Job Corps, U.S. Department of Labor

TEXAS

Capital Area Consortium
Robert E. McPherson, Co-director, The Center for the Study of Human Resources, University of Texas at Austin

Balance of Texas
Robert W. Glover, Acting Director, The Center for the Study of Human Resources, University of Texas at Austin

Contents

*These chapters present the report and recommendations of the Committee on Evaluation of Employment and Training Programs.

List of Tables

List of Figures

Preface

In 1974, the Committee on Evaluation of Employment and Training Programs was established in the National Research Council to assess the political, economic, and social effects of the Comprehensive Employment and Training Act (CETA). Since CETA's enactment, the committee has monitored the introduction of CETA in local governments, the kinds of programs established, changes in delivery systems, and the expansion of public service employment programs. In this study, the committee examines the early effects of the 1978 CETA amendments on public service employment.

Under the original act, management responsibilities for a score of federal employment and training programs for the disadvantaged were transferred to over 400 state and local jurisdictions that were designated as "prime sponsors." The enactment of a countercyclical public service employment program in 1974 began to shift the emphasis in CETA, in terms of funds, from structural to cyclical unemployment programs. CETA appropriations have leaped from $3.7 billion in 1975 to $10 billion in 1979 as CETA has become a major tool attempting to deal with both economic problems and the development of human resources.

Among the issues addressed by the committee in previous reports (see list on page iii) are the effectiveness of local governments in operating decentralized programs within a broad framework of federal policy, the effectiveness of public service employment programs in coping with cyclical joblessness, and the extent to which CETA has mitigated the unemployment problems of the most disadvantaged in our society.

xv

The Comprehensive Employment and Training Act Amendments of 1978 (PL 95-524)—which reauthorized CETA for four years—made a number of significant changes designed to redirect the public service employment programs toward the disadvantaged, emphasize the transition of CETA participants into unsubsidized jobs, lower wage levels, and provide training and other employability development services for persons in public service employment jobs. The act also required increased monitoring and compliance activities. This report does not attempt to evaluate the merits of congressional objectives, but assesses the degree to which public service employment and administration objectives have been achieved.

The assessment of the effects of the CETA amendments is based largely on data obtained from a survey of 28 sample prime sponsors conducted by field research associates who have been monitoring developments in those areas for several years. The sample was drawn from a universe of prime sponsors, stratified by type of sponsor (six cities, nine counties, nine consortia, and four states), by size, and by unemployment rate. The study also drew on statistical data and reports from the Employment and Training Administration and from other sources (see Appendix B for a description of the sample and methodology).

To provide early feedback to policy makers and program managers, the survey was launched in June 1979, two months after the effective date of the new legislation—too soon to capture the full impact of the program changes, but still useful for early indications of trends. Chapter 1 (Overview) and Chapter 7 (Findings and Recommendations) are the report of the Committee on Evaluation of Employment and Training Programs. The remaining chapters are the staff report that provided the supporting data and analysis.

This project, funded by a grant from the Employment and Training Administration of the Department of Labor, is part of the program of the Assembly of Behavioral and Social Sciences of the National Research Council. William Mirengoff, who originated the project, is the study director, and is assisted by Lester Rindler, Harry Greenspan, Scott Seablom, and Lois Black. The authors are indebted to the resident field research associates, to CETA administrators and other officials in the study areas, and to individuals in the Department of Labor who provided statistical data and other helpful materials. The study owes much to the encouragement of Seymour Brandwein, Director, Office of Program Evaluation, U.S. Department of Labor, who contributed to the formulation of the study objectives and provided technical advice. We particularly wish to acknowledge the invaluable contributions of Albert J. Angebranndt in the design of the study and in the review of draft materials.

Support services were provided by Marian D. Miller, Diane Goldman, and Susan Kendall.

I am grateful to the members of the Committee on Evaluation of Employment and Training Programs, who provided guidance for the project, reviewed successive drafts of the report, and participated in the process of formulating recommendations. The committee's recommendations are found in Chapter 7 and are summarized in Chapter 1.

PHILIP J. RUTLEDGE, *Chairman*
Committee on Evaluation of Employment
   and Training Programs

1 Overview

BACKGROUND

The 1978 amendments to the Comprehensive Employment and Training Act (CETA) are the latest in a series of legislative revisions enacted in response to changing economic, social, and political conditions. These modifications reflect a congressional commitment to improve the effectiveness of the CETA programs while ensuring congruence between national objectives and local practices.

The underlying rationale for an employment and training policy is the recognition of the need for governmental intervention in the labor market processes on behalf of the poor and the disadvantaged. During the 1960s, this national policy to intervene was expressed in a profusion of federally controlled programs authorized by the Manpower Development and Training Act and the Economic Opportunity Act.

Enacted in 1973, CETA combined many of these categorical programs into a single block grant and transferred responsibility for their administration from the federal to the state and local governments. These local units of government were to provide employment, training, and remedial services primarily for the structurally unemployed—those who, because of

This chapter presents the summary report of the Committee on Evaluation of Employment and Training Programs.

1

inadequate education, lack of skills, or other structural impediments, are at a disadvantage in the labor market. The public service employment (PSE) program (Title II), which provided federal funds for state and local governments to create temporary jobs for the unemployed in areas of substantial unemployment, was only a minor component of the original legislation.

However, during the recession of 1974, CETA was pressed into service as part of a strategy for combating rising unemployment, and the emphasis of the act began to shift to countercyclical PSE programs. In December 1974, Congress passed the Emergency Jobs and Unemployment Assistance Act, adding a new countercyclical PSE program (Title VI) to CETA and authorizing $2.5 billion to create 250,000 additional positions for one year. Faced with persistently high levels of unemployment, Congress extended Title VI in 1976, and in 1977-1978 expanded PSE as part of a national program to stimulate the economy (Figure 1). In 1977-1978, nearly $8 billion was appropriated to fund 725,000 jobs under Titles II and VI. By 1978, CETA no longer was primarily a program for the structurally unemployed; public service jobs programs accounted for over 60 percent of all CETA expenditures (Figure 2).

The expansion of PSE programs, however, brought in its wake several intractable problems: persons on the lower rungs of the socioeconomic ladder did not participate in adequate numbers; CETA funds were used for activities that otherwise would have been supported by local resources (substitution); and allegations of PSE program abuses aroused skepticism about the program. To some extent these problems reflect the inherent difficulties of achieving congruence in a decentralized program between the objectives of the federal government and the priorities of local officials who administer the programs. However, these difficulties have been aggravated by ambiguous legislation, competing statutory objectives, and pressures for speedy program implementation. The amendments of 1976 attempted to deal with some of these chronic problems but did not produce the desired results.

The amendments of 1978 that reauthorized the CETA legislation are the most recent efforts to address the shortcomings of the PSE programs and appear to be the most effective. This study provides a preliminary assessment of the effects of the reauthorization act on PSE programs. It not only examines these programs to determine whether the goals of the CETA amendments are being attained but also assesses the effects of the reauthorization act on planning and management systems, administrative processes, and institutional relationships.

A word of caution is needed. The field survey, which is the source of much of the information gathered for the study, was conducted during

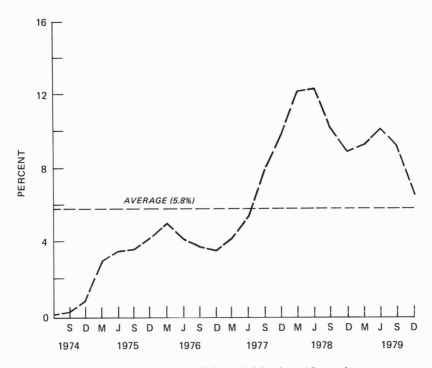

SOURCE: Based on Data from Employment and Training Administration and Bureau of Labor Statistics

FIGURE 1　CETA Public Service Employment as a Percent of the Total Number of Unemployed

June and July 1979, eight months after the enactment of the amendments but only two months after important provisions went into effect. The timing of the survey, although useful for detecting problems and identifying trends, prevented identification of the long-term effects of the reauthorization amendments.

CONGRESSIONAL INTENT

The reauthorization act of 1978 reaffirmed the original goal of CETA, " . . . to provide job training and employment opportunities for economically disadvantaged, unemployed, and underemployed persons" (PL 95-524, Sect. 2). Additionally, the PSE provisions were designed to attain several specific objectives: (1) to increase the share of PSE jobs for persons whose needs for labor market assistance were greatest, (2) to eliminate the

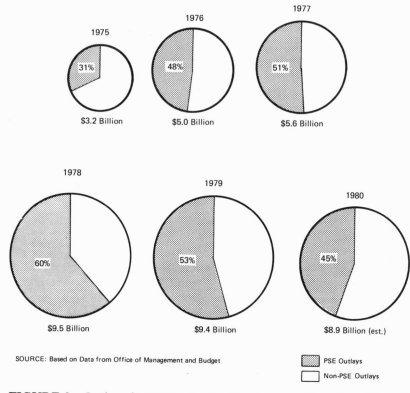

FIGURE 2 Outlays for Public Service Employment Rose from 30 to 60 Percent of All CETA Expenditures by 1978 and Then Declined

use of PSE as a substitute for positions that otherwise would be supported by local funds, (3) to improve the chances of participants succeeding in the labor market by supplementing PSE jobs with training and other supportive services, and (4) to eliminate program abuses. These objectives are not greatly different from earlier aims, but the means used to achieve these elusive ends are radically different. The new legislation relies less on rhetoric and generally worded provisions that nibble at the edges of the problem, and more on stringent requirements and self-enforcing devices that will drive the program in the direction Congress intended.

The 1978 PSE provisions of CETA restrict eligibility, wage levels, and duration of employment for PSE jobs. They also mandate two public service employment programs: one to counter cyclical unemployment; the other to serve the structurally unemployed. Training and employability development services are prescribed for persons in the structural PSE programs and emphasized for those in countercyclical PSE.

The act also attempted to improve the administration of CETA programs. The planning and grant application system was redesigned, tighter procedures for verifying the eligibility of participants and fixing liability for improper enrollment were established, and independent monitoring units were required in each local prime sponsor area to ensure compliance with the act (see chart, p. 6).

EARLY EFFECTS OF THE REAUTHORIZATION ACT

Early indications are that the overriding objective of CETA—to serve more fully those whose needs are greatest—is being achieved. Additionally, wages are lower; the tenure of PSE participants is being shortened; more emphasis is being placed on the transition of enrollees into regular jobs; and prime sponsors are administering programs with a greater concern for accountability. There is also some basis for believing that the incentives for substituting federal funds for local revenues are weaker. However, other goals of the act such as simplifying the planning process and establishing two distinct PSE programs serving different clienteles had not been realized at the time of our survey. Moreover, sponsors had not yet faced up to the full implications of providing training and employability development services for PSE enrollees, and monitoring units were not fully operational in most jurisdictions.

In many areas, one set of goals was achieved at the expense of other objectives. Thus, although the wage and eligibility restrictions helped to increase the share of PSE jobs going to the disadvantaged, they limited the kinds of jobs and services that could be undertaken and often precluded activities favored by local officials. The act has also affected the administration of PSE programs by significantly adding to the administrative burdens of a system that was already straining to keep up with its load.

Serving the Disadvantaged

Early reports indicate that public service employment programs are serving more economically disadvantaged persons, women, youth, blacks, and persons without a high school diploma than they did in the past. The hiring of veterans, however, is down, and welfare recipients are not being selected in numbers anywhere near their proportion in the eligible population.

SUMMARY OF THE COMPREHENSIVE
EMPLOYMENT AND TRAINING ACT (CETA)

The Comprehensive Employment and Training Act Amendments of 1978 (PL 95-524) reauthorized the Comprehensive Employment and Training Act of 1973 (PL 93-203) for fiscal 1979-1982. As amended, CETA has eight titles:

Title I contains administrative provisions. Cities and counties of 100,000 or more and consortia are designated "prime sponsors"; state governments are prime sponsors for balance-of-state areas. Prime sponsors must submit an acceptable plan to the secretary of labor, prepared in consultation with local advisory councils. Participation is limited to 30 months; 18 months for public service employment programs. Allowances and wage limits are specified. Prime sponsors must establish monitoring units. The secretary of labor is required to set performance standards and to establish an Office of Management Assistance. Other provisions deal with the protection of employed workers, nondiscrimination in selection of clients, and prohibition of political activities.

Title II authorizes prime sponsors to provide training, work experience, and supportive services to increase the employability of the economically disadvantaged, unemployed, and underemployed. Part C authorizes assistance to employers for upgrading low-skilled employees. Part D authorizes temporary public service jobs for welfare recipients and for the low-income, long-term unemployed. A portion of allotted funds must be reserved for training. Average wages are set at $7,200 for 1979, with adjustments among areas. CETA wages may not be supplemented above the fixed maximum.

Title III authorizes nationally administered programs for Indians, migrant and seasonal farm workers, older workers, and other groups in need of such services. Part B requires the secretary of labor to develop a comprehensive program of research and evaluation, experimental and demonstration projects, and labor market information, including job banks and occupational information.

Title IV authorizes the Job Corps and summer youth programs; it extends for two years the Youth Employment Demonstration Projects Act programs, enacted in 1977.

Title V establishes the National Commission for Employment Policy, charged with identifying goals, evaluating manpower development programs, and making recommendations to the president and the Congress.

Title VI authorizes temporary public service jobs for the long-term, low-income unemployed and welfare recipients when the national unemployment rate exceeds 4 percent. A portion of the funds must be used for training and employability counseling. Average wages are fixed at $7,200 (for 1979) with area adjustments. Hiring agencies may supplement wages for participants by up to 10 percent of the maximum CETA wage.

Title VII authorizes a two-year demonstration program to test methods for increasing the participation of private businesses in CETA programs for the economically disadvantaged. Prime sponsors are to establish advisory Private Industry Councils with representation from business, labor, education, and the community.

Title VIII authorizes the employment of youth in conservation and other public projects.

Since the eligibility criteria for Titles IID and VI are now similar, the differences between the clienteles of the countercyclical and counterstructural programs are becoming blurred.

Wages, Jobs, and Services

No change in the reauthorization act caused as much consternation among local sponsors as did the reduction in the average wage permitted for PSE jobs. CETA requires that PSE workers be paid prevailing wages, but because the new average PSE wage levels are often below the prevailing wages for public service positions, sponsors are having difficulties in establishing PSE jobs. To adjust to the restrictions, most prime sponsors will shift from high-skill positions to laborer, clerical, and service jobs. Some have been restructuring positions. As a result, most of the administrators in the study sample believe that the usefulness of PSE services has been adversely affected.

This report does not attempt to measure the extent to which the reauthorization act has reduced the practice of using CETA funds for activities that would otherwise be supported by local revenues. It would require an army of auditors to track the federal dollars through 473 prime sponsor budgets. However, there are grounds for believing that the provisions of the new legislation have nudged the program closer to this goal: participants are less qualified, the proportion of professional and skilled positions is being reduced, and the tenure of PSE enrollees is limited.

Transition to Unsubsidized Employment

The reauthorization act of 1978 revives the emphasis on the temporary nature of PSE programs and the necessity for PSE enrollees to move on to regular jobs. Although limits on duration of participation have generated pressure to find unsubsidized jobs for enrollees who must be terminated, it is too early to assess the full impact of the reauthorization act on transition.

An analysis of the methods that sponsors use to promote transition suggests that better results may be obtained when transition planning, centralized placement units, coordination with the employment service, and job development are part of the placement process. The most frequently cited weaknesses in the sponsors' placement systems were inadequate planning and a lack of trained staff.

Program Monitoring

Congress tried, in several ways, to safeguard the integrity of PSE and overcome the negative image resulting from allegations of fraud and abuse. Early indications are that some efforts were successful; others have yet to be tested. By assigning liability for improper enrollment to prime sponsors, setting sanctions for noncompliance, and requiring intensified monitoring, the amendments have made program managers more concerned about preventing program abuses. Much stricter methods are being used to screen applicants for eligibility, and prime sponsor efforts often exceed those required by the legislation. There is, however, some uncertainty as to how the liability provisions will be implemented.

Sponsors have been slow in establishing independent monitoring units and unsure about their roles. Moreover, there is some question about the independence of the units that have been established—virtually all of them are appointed by and are responsible to the local CETA administrators.

At the federal level, monitoring has been stepped up and preventive programs have been initiated, but these activities have been hampered by staff and funding limitations.

Planning and Administration

The redirection of the CETA programs has exacted a price. Most of the 1978 amendments, aimed at strengthening the program and ensuring compliance with national policies, have generated a host of complex administrative tasks.

Although Congress attempted to simplify the grant application process by replacing separate annual plans with a master plan and annual supplements, sponsors are finding the new planning documents no less difficult than the old and, in any event, no more useful for local operations and evaluation. In other respects, the administration of PSE programs is becoming more complex. Sponsors identify the wage, eligibility, and training provisions as especially difficult to implement.

Sponsors have tried to minimize the strains created by the new requirements by adapting them to existing systems and practices. Nevertheless, a substantial number of prime sponsor organizations have been badly shaken by the added complexities and funding uncertainties.

Conclusions

The two major forces driving the PSE program in the direction that Congress has charted are the wage and eligibility provisions of the reauthorization act. The wage provisions are forcing prime sponsors to eliminate or restructure high-wage PSE positions. The jobs that result from these changes require lower skills and are therefore less attractive to persons with alternative employment opportunities but more accessible to persons with limited qualifications. The wage provisions also tend to discourage substitution by reducing the number of professional and skilled positions that are the most susceptible to this practice. The stiffer eligibility criteria not only increase the share of disadvantaged persons participating in PSE programs, but also tend to reduce the proclivity of sponsors to use PSE workers instead of their regular workforce to provide essential public services.

Balancing competing objectives is an inherent problem of legislation that pursues multiple goals, and CETA is liberally sprinkled with such goals. The pursuit of one objective may require the abandonment of another. Thus, the enrollment of the most disadvantaged may limit the kinds of services that sponsors can provide and may adversely affect the quality of these services. Similarly, the limited qualifications of PSE workers may reduce the likelihood of their being placed in unsubsidized jobs.

Perhaps the goal that has remained most elusive is that of combining training and other employability development services with PSE jobs. To a large extent, PSE is still operating as an income maintenance program for the unemployed and a welcome supplement to local government services. There are, to be sure, inevitable difficulties in meshing programs that are subject to different rules and institutional frameworks. However, the basic question is whether, without training and other employability services, the kinds of experience afforded by PSE programs—largely in public works and parks—contribute to the participant's ability to compete in the labor market.

SUMMARY OF RECOMMENDATIONS

The Committee on Evaluation of Employment and Training Programs (CETP) proposes that sweeping legislative changes in the PSE program be deferred unless such changes are necessitated by rapid increases in unemployment. The employment and training system, battered by successive waves of program changes, needs, above all else, a period of consolidation and stability. For this reason, the major recommendations summarized below are primarily technical proposals that may help to facilitate the implementation of the new CETA. A full discussion of these and other recommendations is presented in Chapter 7.

1. *Eligibility Criteria.* The new eligibility criteria appear to be accomplishing the congressional objective of focusing PSE programs on the disadvantaged and should be retained. However, in the event of a significant rise in unemployment, the Title VI criteria should be reassessed to determine whether they are sufficiently broad for an expanded counterrecessionary program.

2. *Target Groups.* The act designates so many groups for special consideration that these designations cannot be used effectively for targeting. The committee recommends that Congress reserve special consideration for fewer groups so as to provide a better basis for establishing priorities. More effective methods should be devised for recruiting and enrolling target groups, especially public welfare recipients.

3. *Wages.* Although the wage provisions of the reauthorization act complicate the task of operating PSE programs, they appear to be effective in accomplishing the basic objectives of CETA and should be retained until their full effects can be weighed. Some minor modifications, however, are recommended: (1) the method used to adjust the national average wage for local areas should be modified to give greater weight to government wages; (2) in areas where permissible PSE wages are generally below prevailing rates for government positions, additional wage supplementation should be permitted; and (3) the PSE maximum wages should be modified annually to adjust for wage escalation.

4. *Transition of Enrollees.* Efforts to enhance the employability of enrollees or to find unsubsidized work for those terminating should be supported more vigorously by the Department of Labor. The Department of Labor should provide sponsors with models of employability development plans, assistance in developing staff capabilities in job placement procedures, and better labor market information that is more useful for placement activities.

5. *The Planning System.* The Department of Labor should increase assistance to prime sponsors, program agents, and other subjurisdictions to improve the quality of plans. Training sessions and materials should provide information on the principles and methodology of planning. Furthermore, the Department of Labor, in consultation with prime sponsors, should establish a task force to review the present guidelines for the purpose of culling out requirements for nonessential data.

6. *Program Monitoring.* The Department of Labor should review the monitoring activities of all levels of administration to clarify the role of each and to integrate monitoring activities. At the regional level, technical assistance should be provided by individuals who have no responsibilities for monitoring activities. Furthermore, the DOL should clarify its policy on liability for ineligible applicants.

7. *Program Administration.* Congress should use the authority available under the act for advance funding to permit more orderly planning and management and to provide more lead time for implementing legislative changes. Although the PSE programs have not yet exceeded statutory administrative cost limits, the DOL should review the additional tasks mandated by the reauthorization act to determine their impact on costs and staffing.

8. *Employment Service/CETA Relations.* The need for closer relationships between the employment service and prime sponsors has been generally recognized. To derive the greatest benefit from the special competencies of both systems, incentives should be provided to encourage close coordination in job development and intake activities. The committee also recommends that Congress establish a commission to study the roles and relationships of the employment service and CETA manpower systems and to consider changes in the Wagner-Peyser and CETA legislation that would harmonize the two systems.

ISSUES REQUIRING FURTHER STUDY

This study has focused on the effects of the 1978 amendments on the CETA public service employment programs and on the degree to which the goals of the amendments have been realized. It is apparent, however, that several broader issues warrant further examination: the harmonization of federal and local goals, the limits of decentralized management, PSE wage policy, the relative roles of the private and public sectors in CETA programs, the relationship between CETA and the welfare system, problems of resource allocations, and the institutional roles and relationships of agencies involved with CETA.

Limits of Decentralized Management

The CETA system, originally designed to simplify the employment and training system, has evolved into a jumble of special programs. Even the public service employment programs are comprised of several subparts with different objectives and ground rules. When reauthorization changes were introduced, they had a shattering effect on local sponsors. This has been reflected in low morale, excessive staff turnover, and the break-up of consortium arrangements. Further examination is necessary to ascertain whether the present management systems can adequately administer the CETA legislation.

The cornerstones of CETA, decentralization and decategorization of employment and training programs, began to erode immediately after the enactment of the legislation. New program initiatives to serve special groups and deal with special problems created a new generation of categorical programs. These, plus a growing number of federal specifications, have substantially increased the federal presence, which is a continuing source of tension among the various levels of government responsible for program administration. The reauthorization act reinforced the trend towards more categorical programs and greater central control. After six years of trial and error, the limits of decentralization and decategorization in a human resources program and the roles of the participating institutions should be reexamined.

The issue of congruence between national and local objectives has been discussed in earlier reports of the CETP (National Research Council 1978, 1980). Since it lies at the heart of many CETA conceptual and operating problems, it bears repeating.

The underlying assumption of a decentralized program is that national and local goals are closely matched. In fact, however, they diverge significantly. CETA embodies a blend of federal, state, and local aspirations with each participant trying to shape the program to meet its own needs. Local deviation from federal goals, however, invites federal restrictions that, in turn, narrow local flexibility. The reauthorization amendments reflect the congressional perception that local programs have not adequately responded to national purposes. Local sponsors, on the other hand, view such restrictions as onerous and an encroachment on their freedom to make local program decisions. In their view the CETA amendments "have brought the program back to Washington." Central to this issue is the need to establish a balance between federal and local needs.

Wages for PSE Jobs

Although PSE wage restrictions increase the participation of the least advantaged, encourage transition, and deter substitution, these restrictions are frequently not compatible with the prevailing wage requirement of CETA and may have unintended effects. Several questions should be addressed: Does the wage policy threaten the established job classification and wage standards in the public sector? Does it reduce the incentives for unemployment insurance and welfare beneficiaries to accept PSE jobs? Does it substitute "make-work" activities for useful public services? Most importantly, do the jobs that are established under the new wage policy contribute to the job potential of PSE participants?

Private and Public Sector Roles

Prior to the reauthorization act, federally supported on-the-job training in private industry was one of several program options available to prime sponsors, but was used infrequently. The new private industry councils (PICs) and the targeted jobs tax credit program were designed to stimulate greater participation of the private sector in training and expanding employment opportunities for the disadvantaged. At issue are the respective roles of the private and public sectors in the CETA programs. It is not yet clear whether the private sector role can be enlarged enough to significantly lessen reliance on the public sector, especially in the event of an economic slowdown.

CETA and the Welfare System

The administration's proposed welfare reform bill contains a jobs component that would be implemented through the CETA-PSE programs. The bill, which would establish a new PSE title (IIE), would greatly increase the number of PSE positions available to welfare recipients. CETA experience indicates that employers are sometimes not eager to hire welfare recipients and that the recipients themselves are frequently reluctant to enter PSE programs. At issue are the feasibility of adding 400,000 welfare eligibles to the public service employment program, the ability of the CETA system to absorb the change, the effect of increased use of welfare recipients on the level of public services that can be provided, and the capability of the CETA system to provide the training and other supportive services needed by these PSE participants.

Resource Allocations

The reauthorization act has revised the formulas for allocating resources for the comprehensive manpower programs in Title IIA, B, and C and the public service employment programs in Title IID: it has also introduced new formulas for youth programs and private sector initiatives. The effects of the new formulas on the distribution of resources should be explored in terms of equity considerations, and differences in resource needs stemming from geographic variations in labor market conditions, wage levels, and service costs.

Objectives of Public Service Employment

Attention needs to be given at the national level to defining what it is that CETA PSE is intended to accomplish and to adopting a program design consistent with that objective. Many of the problems that have occurred under CETA can be traced to congressional vacillation and a failure to define a clear and consistent set of objectives for CETA. Questions that need to be addressed include: Can public service employment be a program for all seasons? Can it simultaneously be effective as a countercyclical device, as a vehicle for training the structurally unemployed, as a tool for income maintenance, and as a means of assisting financially hard-pressed state and local governments?

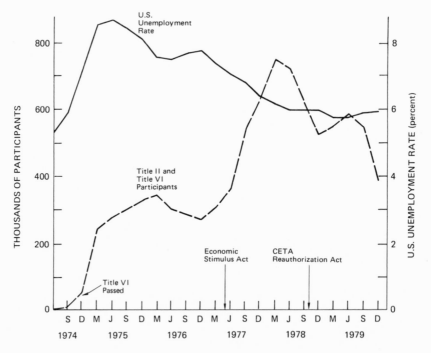

SOURCE: Based on Data from Employment and Training Administration and Bureau of Labor Statistics

FIGURE 3   CETA Public Service Employment Levels Do Not Match Changes in Unemployment Rates

Public Service Employment as a Countercyclical Measure

Timing is an important element of fiscal policy. For PSE to be an effective part of a countercyclical strategy, the jobs must be filled quickly at the onset of a recession and phased out when the stimulus is no longer needed. However, the experiences with PSE programs show little evidence of this kind of fine tuning (Figure 3). Although the 1978 amendments authorized a "trigger" to adjust the scale of Title VI programs to the rate of unemployment, this mechanism has not been used.

The wage and eligibility restrictions of the reauthorization act may retard a rapid job creation buildup during a recession, while delays in phasing down the program in a recovery period may contribute to inflationary pressures.

If Title VI is to serve as an effective weapon in the arsenal of fiscal policy, consideration should be given to developing a PSE design that will facilitate rapid expansion and timely reduction and is administratively feasible.

More specifically, the concept and design of the "trigger" should be reexamined in the light of the complexities of inflation accompanied by high unemployment.

2 Planning and Administration

The 1978 amendments to the Comprehensive Employment and Training Act (CETA) are the most radical revision of the legislation since its enactment in 1973. The amendments, designed to buttress weaknesses in the legislation and to ensure local compliance with national policies, included new and detailed prescriptions that have made administration of the program more difficult and have reduced national and local flexibility.

This chapter explores the effects of the 1978 legislation on the planning and administrative systems for operating public service jobs programs at the local level and examines changes in institutional relationships, particularly those involving federal and local officials.

When CETA was renewed in 1978, Congress made a number of significant changes. Programs were added to involve private employers more directly and to permit upgrading of employed workers. Experimental youth programs, enacted in 1977, were incorporated into CETA. The planning system was revised to reduce paperwork and broaden participation on planning councils. Steps were taken to discourage the substitution of CETA for local public service employees. Congress assigned liability for ineligible participants and strengthened monitoring to control program abuse. All of these administrative and program changes affected the management of CETA programs at the local level.

Perhaps most important is the redesign of public service employment programs (PSE), which has made the act unwieldy to manage. Among specific changes in PSE were the establishment of separate programs for the structurally and cyclically unemployed, tightening eligibility criteria, restricting wage levels, limiting the tenure of CETA participants, and combining employability development services with public service jobs.

EFFECT OF REAUTHORIZATION ON THE PLANNING SYSTEM

During the first five years of CETA, the planning and grant-application process had become increasingly complex as new programs were added. The 1978 reauthorization act attempted to simplify the process through reductions in paper flow and through better integration of the planning system. The act also attempted to expand the grass-roots participation in manpower planning. This section reviews the implementation of these changes in the months immediately following the CETA reauthorization and assesses their effect on the planning system.

PLANNING PRIOR TO REAUTHORIZATION

Local manpower planning systems have long been considered essential for the implementation of employment and training legislation. CETA planning was expected to provide (1) an analytical framework for identifying both the populations in need of service and the programs that could, in light of local labor market conditions, best meet the needs of this population; (2) closer consultation among relevant groups in the community; and (3) a systematic way for federal and local officials to check performance against goals and assess the effectiveness of programs and service deliverers.

However, the CETA planning system never totally fulfilled its promise. As new programs were added for public service employment, youth, and other special purposes, planning became fragmented and plans became little more than a series of separate grant applications that were repeatedly modified to reflect program or budget changes. Although plans brought together management information, they generally did not meet the more strategic, long-range goals of relating programs to the employment and training needs of the community or the management needs of local administrators.

CETA plans for Title II and Title VI primarily consisted of lists of jobs to be filled, wages to be paid, and numbers of participants to be hired. They also contained stock "assurances" that local officials would observe regulations pertaining to wages, selection of participants, conditions of employment, protection of standards and rights of regular workers, and maintenance of effort.

For CETA programs generally and for public service employment most particularly, program decisions and formal plans were often unrelated. In fiscal 1977, for example, the Department of Labor (DOL), as a measure to stimulate the economy, required prime sponsors to set new and higher enrollment goals for public service employment programs long after the original plans for the year had been approved. Although the trappings of a planning system were retained, the revised plan merely reflected decisions already made.

Thus, plans before the reauthorization were used more as a justification for budgets than as a basis for designing rational local employment and training programs. Plans had become a collection of grant applications and, as such, were treated perfunctorily at the local level.

PLANNING UNDER THE REAUTHORIZATION ACT

One of the objectives that Congress hoped to achieve through the reauthorization act was a simplification of the planning process. Congress sought to reduce paperwork, broaden participation in advisory councils, promote the independence of these councils, and encourage comprehensive area-wide planning (U.S. Congress, 1978b, p. 14; 1978a, p. 5).

The most sweeping change was the replacement of separate annual plans for each title by a one-time master plan (a long-term agreement between the sponsor and the Department of Labor) and an annual plan covering all programs operated by the sponsor. The change was intended to simplify planning documents by no longer requiring resubmission of information that did not change from year to year. This section seeks to ascertain whether plans have in fact been simplified and, more importantly, whether they are more useful for program development.

A comparison of past and present requirements showed that, despite the intent to reduce paperwork, new plans, if prepared according to DOL instructions, must contain significantly more detail. For example, a description of the industrial and occupational composition of the labor market and of economic trends was required for the pre-reauthorization Prime Sponsor Agreements, whereas the new master plans must include detailed current demand data by major occupations and industries, and projections of demand over the next five years. Current master plans must also contain more detailed information on the eligible population, delivery agencies, coordination, administration, and management.

Similarly, requirements for the annual plans under the reauthorization act do not reduce the volume of information. The annual plan is integrated in appearance only; it actually has several subparts, each of which deals with a separate title or program. For example, there are eight separate titles or subtitles for which the demographic characteristics of the eligible populations must be provided; less detail was required for the annual supplements before reauthorization. The new annual plans must also include a detailed description of each public service employing agency, including information on the level of employment not supported under CETA, layoffs that have occurred or are anticipated, and hiring and promotional freezes. This information is necessary for monitoring maintenance of effort, but it imposes a heavy data-gathering burden on local officials. Moreover, PSE budget information must be estimated separately for project and nonproject employment on a quarterly basis; formerly only combined figures were required.

In summary, both the master and annual plans must contain much more detailed information than was contained in pre-reauthorization plans. These new information requirements, based in part on legislation, are intended to strengthen surveillance over the CETA system and to broaden the scope and depth of local planning. The result, however, is a more complex planning document.

Reactions to the new planning requirements vary. Sixteen of the twenty-eight planners or sponsors in the NRC survey thought that, under the new requirements, preparation of plans has become more difficult and time-consuming than it had been in the past, while eight believed that the new requirements have made little difference in this respect. Four believed that, in time, information would be accumulated and consolidated, and that planning under the revised system would then become easier than it had been under the former system.

Those who found 1980 plans more difficult noted in particular the lack of source data for statistical profiles of the eligible population and labor market information. This information is not available in sufficient geographic detail on a current basis. Another time-consuming requirement is the occupational summaries of projected public service employment slots. In the compilation for the balance of North Carolina, for example, more than 10,000 positions were listed. Sponsors questioned the need for such detail, particularly since they are not bound by occupations listed. The exercise, in their view, does not necessarily contribute to program decisions.

Far more serious, however, is the recurrent problem that results from delays in appropriations and the need to adjust plans to revised allocations when appropriations are announced. Sponsors began the fiscal 1980 planning cycle in May 1979, based on the administration's fiscal 1980 budget. When the 1980 appropriations were enacted in October, funding levels were changed sharply, necessitating revisions in plans. Because the level of funding is not known when plans are being drawn, the amount of detail that is required of plans is unrealistic.[1]

Other sponsor complaints were the time pressures of the planning cycle and the programmatic changes that make projections difficult. For example, the restructuring of PSE positions due to wage limitations affects the program, but local officials were not in a position to fully evaluate these changes during the planning period.

Despite the intent to simplify the planning documents, plans still contain hundreds of pages. Presumably benefits will accrue in the future because, except for sections on labor market information, the master plan will not need to be revised. However, grant modifications are likely to continue unless the appropriation and allocation system can be made more stable.

Reporting

The presumed saving in the paperwork for planning is more than offset by the new reporting requirements. The reauthorization act calls for a new annual evaluation report that is more extensive than the regular quarterly reports. Although this detailed information may be useful for program evaluation, the benefits are not readily apparent to the majority of prime sponsors interviewed. Eight of the sponsors saw some potential advantage, mainly because the new requirements necessitate a shift to automated data processing that can provide better access to program data; but 16 felt there was no immediate improvement in their evaluation capability. The remaining four sponsors were not able to respond since the new annual reports were not required at the time of the interview. Two respondents who used their own information systems for program evaluation and decision making believed that the increased statistical information would be used only by the Department of Labor.

As a result of the new reporting load, the quality of regular quarterly program statistics may suffer. At present there is no consistency in the way sponsors report many items such as the number of terminations and placements, and even the number enrolled. Moreover, enrollees who were transferred among titles were frequently counted among new enrollees and terminees. Hence, transfers overstate the number of enrollees and the number of terminees, making it difficult to arrive at placement rates and cost estimates.

Usefulness of Plans

The enormous amount of time invested in compiling statistical and financial data might be justified if the resulting plans serve the needs of local administrators or aid federal officials in supervising local programs.

Eleven of the twenty-eight sponsors in the study sample thought that the new plans are potentially more useful to them for PSE operations than were earlier plans, but fifteen believed that the usefulness of plans remained unchanged, and two felt that it was too early in the planning cycle to make a judgment.

Most sponsors interviewed indicated that the new planning documents, despite problems in the data, provide better targeting information than those of the past. There was less agreement that the new plans will be more useful for other operating purposes such as allocating resources among agencies and subjurisdictions, selecting employers and PSE positions, and planning for the transition of enrollees to unsubsidized employment. Nor was there agreement on the usefulness of the new plans for evaluating PSE programs. Two-thirds of the regional office representatives interviewed reported that planning documents were useful for program review and administrative control. The additional detail on systems and processes required in the new planning documents was believed to be more useful than in the past. However, several of these respondents felt that they could only use a fraction of the information available.

On the whole, plans are mainly useful as an organized way of documenting and justifying local operations. Although plans are better structured than in the past, it is questionable whether they are more relevant for operations and evaluation because there is little relationship between program plans and supporting economic and demographic data. Major decisions relating to public service employment programs are based on available funds, enrollment time schedules, the needs of government agencies, and political judgments on resource allocations. Planning documents frequently play little or no part in these decisions. However, the process of putting together the planning documents requires interaction among administrative and elected officials, program operators, and members of the planning council that contributes to the objective of broadening participation in decision making.

EFFECT OF REAUTHORIZATION ON DECISION MAKING

Councils

The reauthorization act attempted to revitalize local manpower advisory councils by broadening their composition. Before reauthorization, membership was balanced among client groups, program service deliverers, business and labor, elected officials, public agencies, and other groups (National Research Council 1978, p. 58).[2] The amendments of 1978 specified the addition of more client groups—unorganized labor, agricultural workers, veterans, and the handicapped—as well as institutions whose activities are closely related to CETA—public welfare and vocational education agencies.

In our study, 16 of the 28 sponsors reported that representatives of these groups had been or would soon be appointed to the local councils. Responding to the act's emphasis on the private sector and special target groups, several sponsors also added employers and women's representatives to the councils.

There was no immediate sign, however, that the addition of new members significantly altered the councils' role. In 14 areas, either no change or a decline in council influence was reported. In 9 areas, council influence was reported to be greater since reauthorization, but in most cases this change resulted not from the amendments but rather from more active participation of council members or the activation of subcommittees; several of these respondents attributed greater council influence to the addition of business representatives or the appointment of an independent chairman—changes that are linked to reauthorization. In the remaining 5 areas, respondents believed that judgment would be premature.

In recognition of the fact that five-sixths of all jobs are in the private sector, the CETA reauthorization act sought to increase the role of private business and industry in CETA by requiring that Private Industry Councils (PICs) be established in each area to augment on-the-job training and initiate new approaches for combining training with work experience in the private sector. To avoid duplication of other CETA programs, PICs were to develop their activities in consultation with prime sponsors. Sixteen of the twenty-eight sponsors in the study sample had established PICs and arranged for consultation with PIC councils.[3] Several of these reported that the delineation of roles between the regular advisory councils and PICs was still unsettled. An Ohio State University study based on a review of 25 prime sponsors also concludes that progress is being made in establishing the organizational framework for private sector initiative programs, but in 9 of 21 cases in which a PIC has been functioning, tensions exist between PIC and CETA staff over the degree of autonomy afforded to the PIC (Ohio State University Research Foundation, 1979b, pp. 15-16).

PSE Decision Making

The NRC survey confirms that the decision-making process in public service employment programs remains essentially unchanged. The CETA administrator, armed with knowledge of the complex rules and procedures, plays a central role. Basic decisions on allocation of slots among jurisdictions and employing agencies are made by the CETA administrator, often in consultation with elected officials or with planning councils. Decisions on selection of target groups are even more likely to be handled by the CETA staff.

Decision making in consortia and "balance of states" is more complex because of multiple jurisdictions and administrative layers. Key operational decisions are made largely at the subjurisdiction level.[4] In the Orange County Consortium, for example, selections of employing agencies, positions, and projects are made by program agents, whereas the prime sponsor is most influential in selection of target groups. In Maine, Title IID programs are approved at the county level, while Title VI projects are referred to the balance-of-state prime sponsor with recommendations from local councils. In the balance of Texas, an area with over 130 counties, all PSE program decisions, except for selection of target groups, are made by councils of governments and community action agencies that operate the subarea programs.

Although the major decision-making processes for CETA programs have not yet been affected significantly by the reauthorization, three factors directly related to the act may affect decision making in the future: (1) the requirement that the chairman of the council be a public member and that the sponsor provide supporting staff for councils; (2) the emergence of PICs as an influential factor; and (3) the feedback of information from program monitoring. But more important to PSE decision making are external factors such as major shifts in program funds and the specificity of the act itself, which narrows the range of prime sponsor decisions. While local decisions are always based on nationally determined appropriations, major changes in funding levels made after allotments are announced, in effect, tend to limit local discretion.

EFFECT OF REAUTHORIZATION ON ADMINISTRATION

ORGANIZATIONAL STRUCTURES AND SYSTEMS

The transition from the old to the new CETA sent shock waves through the system; some prime sponsors were better able to absorb them than others. Measures aimed at strengthening programs, making them more consistent with national policies, improving performance, and preventing abuse add considerably to the administrative load. On the whole, however, the reauthorization act has had more effect on processes than on the basic organizational structures and systems for handling CETA programs. The institutional framework that had been established for carrying out CETA responsibilities remained largely intact.

CETA organizations vary in complexity depending on their scale of operations and whether they serve a single jurisdiction or multiple jurisdictions. Eighteen of the twenty-eight CETA offices in the study report directly to elected officials—mayors, county commissioners or executives, or governors. In the remaining 10 areas, including most cities, the CETA administration is lodged in a human resources department or other umbrella agency. None of the sponsors in the survey reported changes in the organizational location of CETA staffs following reauthorization although several expected that changes would result from the dissolution or formation of consortia.

Most of the prime sponsors surveyed either contract out all activities, retaining only central office functions for the CETA administrator's staff, or have a mixed pattern with some functions contracted out and others performed directly by the CETA administrator's staff. These arrangements were not affected by the reauthorization.

Nor did the new legislation affect the assignment of PSE functions. In two-thirds of the surveyed areas, these activities are under the supervision of the CETA administrator or the chief of operations; in the remaining areas the activities of the public service employment programs are handled with other comparable activities by functional units. In consortia, balance of states, or large counties, some PSE activities are carried out at more local levels. Only one area—the Pinellas–St. Petersburg consortium— reported a major internal reorganization clearly associated with the reauthorization. The CETA administrative office was restructured along functional lines to handle new activities such as eligibility verification, monitoring, and keeping track of the lengths of time that individuals have participated in the program.

Although the basic patterns tend to persist, changes occur frequently for reasons not related to legislation. At the time of the survey, 11 of 28 prime sponsors were in the midst of major reorganizations. In Texas, an incoming governor reduced and consolidated the balance-of-state staff as part of a state-wide personnel cut. The staff of Lorain County, Ohio, was also cut drastically to lower administrative costs and improve management. Cleveland, the major consortium in the sample, was on the verge of dissolution because of interjurisdictional and management problems, and two other consortia in the sample (Austin and Raleigh) were experiencing internal tensions.[5] Calhoun County, Michigan, was negotiating a consortium agreement with Barry County and was in the process of taking over the activities of a community action agency. Long Beach was being reorganized and expanded to integrate a welfare demonstration program with CETA. Several other prime sponsors were expecting changes due to turnover of key personnel.

In summary, although the widespread strains and tensions in the CETA system were aggravated by new reauthorization procedures, they did not result in organizational upheavals. Most sponsors adjusted to the changes by beefing up monitoring and record-keeping units and reassigning staff. This is discussed more fully later in this chapter. The major changes that did occur are not attributable to the reauthorization.

PROBLEMS IN ADMINISTERING PSE DURING THE TRANSITION PERIOD

The rigid time table in the reauthorization act, along with changes in funding, new directives, and shifts in program emphasis kept the CETA public service employment program in turmoil throughout most of 1979. Restrictions on eligibility, duration of projects, and tenure of participants went into effect on the day the act was passed in October 1978. Maximum wage provisions and measures to control fraud and abuse became effective 90 days later. The act was to be fully effective on April 1, 1979, only five months after enactment, and in the middle of a program year. Sponsors were faced with the task of establishing mechanisms for determining and verifying eligibility under new rules, tracking the tenure of enrollees, and redesigning PSE activities and jobs to conform with the new wage requirements. Furthermore, while doing all of this, they were to activate monitoring units, arrange for youth projects, and set up private industry councils.

The number one problem during the transition period was converting the new regulations and requirements into operating procedures (Table 1). Wage and eligibility regulations were revised twice, and literally hundreds of field directives, touching on all aspects of the PSE programs, were issued. Despite these communications, sponsors complained that policy direction was absent, interpretations of regulations were confusing, and, in some cases, questions went unanswered. One CETA administrator suspended all PSE hiring pending clarification of instructions. Others were confused by "grandfather" clauses (which permitted continued supplementation of wages for Title IID participants enrolled before October 1978) and other wage provisions. These problems were compounded because sponsors had to communicate rule changes and provide guidance and supervision to program agents and PSE employers in their jurisdictions.

The transition period was characterized by continuous revision of grants to adjust to changes in funding levels and program shifts. First, in early October 1978, sponsors were required to close out and renew existing grants so that the program could continue to operate in fiscal 1979. A

TABLE 1   Problems in Implementing the CETA Reauthorization Provisions During the Transition Period, October 1978 to March 1979, Sample Prime Sponsor Areas

	Percent of Areas	
Activity	Identify Activity as Problem	Consider Problem Most Serious[a]
Converting new regulations and instructions into operating procedures	82	36
Modifying grants	68	14
Installing procedures for determining and verifying eligibility	64	14
Installing systems to record and track tenure of individuals	61	14
Adjusting to changes in funding	57	32
Adjusting to wage provisions, arranging for training, and other activities	50	46

Source: Based on reports from 28 areas.

[a]Some respondents noted more than one problem as most serious.

second round of modifications to adjust for allocations and provisional requirements occurred in December 1978. The DOL then set April 1, 1979, as the deadline for submitting revised fiscal 1979 plans in the format required by the reauthorization act. The fourth cycle, beginning in May 1979, was the preparation of fiscal 1980 plans. The administrative activity involved in revising grants and plans is, in itself, mind-boggling, yet it represents only the tip of the iceberg; corresponding changes were necessary in thousands of subgrants and contracts.

Close to two-thirds of the areas reported that installing systems for determining and verifying eligibility hampered operations during the transition period for two reasons. First, the systems are elaborate and time-consuming (see Chapter 6). Second, the eligibility criteria for programs under Titles IID and VI are only marginally different, and a different set of rules was in effect for part of the transition period.[6]

Most of the sponsors in the study had problems in installing systems to track the length of time enrollees participated in the program. The law provides for a 30-month maximum for all CETA enrollees, but restricts classroom training to 24 months, and tenure in public service jobs to 18 months. Enrollments prior to October 1978 may be counted toward the

PSE limit but not toward the 30-month rule. The maze of rules relating to sequential activities, part-time enrollments, interrupted tenure, periods when the enrollee does not receive allowances or wages, etc., is nearly as complex as that for eligibility.

Other problems during the transition period involved finding positions that met the lower wage requirements and arranging for training PSE workers. These became more acute after April 1, when the act became fully operational (as discussed elsewhere in this chapter).

Adjustment of Funding Levels

Among the most serious problems facing prime sponsors was the continuous adjustment to changes in funding levels and delays in apropriations. Fiscal 1979 began without an appropriation for CETA funds. To sustain the programs, the Department of Labor urged state and local governments to continue operating with unspent funds carried over from the previous year, or, if necessary, with borrowed funds. When the new appropriation was enacted two weeks after the beginning of the year, it required a substantial realignment of PSE programs.

The $5.9 billion PSE appropriation assumed average enrollments (Title II and Title VI combined) of 625,000—a drop of 130,000 from the peak enrollment level of 755,000 in March 1978. The cut was exclusively in Title VI countercyclical PSE programs. Participants in Title IID, the new structural program, were to be twice the number in the 1978 Title II program.

It was soon apparent, however, that the number enrolled was dropping faster than had been expected (Figure 4 and Table 2). When the appropriation was passed, DOL urged an orderly reduction of program levels, despite the fact that the number on board was already below target levels.[7] The biggest drop had actually occurred in the final quarter of the previous fiscal year (July-September 1978) against a backdrop of heated congressional debate on the future of public service employment programs. Clearly, uncertainties concerning funding and the continuation of the program had a paralyzing effect.

For individual sponsors, the important figures are their own allocations. These were sharply different from funds in 1978 for three reasons: (a) appropriations for Title IID increased (as compared with appropriations for Title II), while Title VI funds decreased; (b) the Title IID allocation formula was changed[8]; and (c) area unemployment levels changed. Twenty-three of the twenty-eight areas in the sample received less money than in the prior year, and five areas received more. All received more for Title IID, and all but one received less for Title VI.

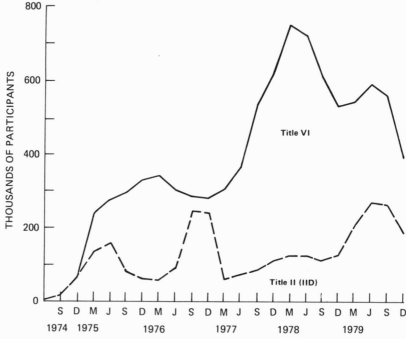

SOURCE: Based on Data from Employment and Training Administration

FIGURE 4   Trends in CETA Public Service Employment

In this atmosphere, sponsors found it hard to plan and carry out orderly programs. Enrollments declined in 18 of 28 areas, and several sponsors suspended recruitment until some of these problems were resolved. By March 1979, 20 of the prime sponsors in the survey were lagging significantly behind planned levels of enrollments or expenditures.

Alarmed by the sharp declines, the DOL launched a drive in March 1979 to boost enrollments to 625,000 by the end of June. Nonetheless, 15 of 28 areas in the study were still below new enrollment goals as of June 1979. With the possibility of reduced appropriations, cautious prime sponsors were reluctant to do any hiring because they feared subsequent layoff problems. Moreover, it was becoming difficult to recruit and process applicants and to establish positions that met wage guidelines (see Chapter 4). Eight of the survey sponsors were threatened with withdrawal of funds because of lagging expenditures.[9] By the end of June, enrollments reached 592,000, about 5 percent below the target level. The alternating pressures

TABLE 2   Participants in Title II (IID) and Title VI, Fiscal 1978-1980 (thousands)

Year and Month	Total Titles II and VI	Title II (IID)	Title VI
FY 1978			
October (1977)	571	100	471
November	603	106	497
December	627	110	517
January (1978)	674	118	556
February	751	128	623
March	752	128	624
April	755	126	629
May	736	125	611
June	729	126	603
July	698	122	576
August	659	118	541
September	608	112	496
Average	680	118	562
FY 1979			
October	554	109	445
November	544	109	435
December	534	118	416
January (1979)	514	155	360
February	526	177	349
March	546	210	336
April	553	242	311
May	561	250	311
June	592	266	326
July	604	272	331
August	604	278	326
September	554	257	297
Average	557	204	354
FY 1980			
October	420	208	211
November	412	202	210
December	395	193	201

Source: Employment and Training Administration, U.S. Department of Labor (unpublished data).

NOTE: Details may not add to totals due to rounding.

to increase and decrease enrollments continued as further program cuts were made in fiscal 1980.[10]

The "Cliff" Problem

The difficulty in maintaining enrollments in fiscal 1979 was underscored in the closing months of the year. Many sponsors, while being pressed by DOL to increase their PSE levels, faced the prospect of laying off large numbers of PSE enrollees who had reached the limits of their tenure. Congressional action to limit the duration of enrollment in PSE programs to 18 months emphasized the transitional nature of PSE as a bridge between unemployment and a regular unsubsidized job. It was expected that these limitations would (1) induce participants to seek unsubsidized employment, (2) encourage employers to absorb PSE workers or assist them in obtaining other permanent jobs, (3) discourage employers from substituting CETA participants for regular employees, and (4) make the PSE program available to the maximum number of unemployed persons (U.S. Congress 1978b, p. 9). Previously, the length of time that enrollees could remain in PSE jobs was unspecified and cases were reported of persons who had been hired under the Emergency Employment Act of 1971 who were still on the CETA payroll. A report by Westat, Inc. (1979, Appendix C, p. C-1) showed that, after 18 months, one-third of PSE participants continued to be employed in CETA jobs.[11]

The reactions of the sponsors in the NRC study to the tenure rule were varied. Few objected to the policy, but some complained about the additional workload that would result from maintaining records of enrollment dates. More important was the problem of dealing with enrollees whose tenure was about to expire. At the time of the survey, nearly all sponsors expected to face a "cliff" problem on October 1, 1979. The act provided that those enrollees who had been in the program for 6 months as of October 1, 1978, could continue to hold PSE positions for 12 more months. In half of the 22 survey areas for which data were available, 50 percent or more of PSE enrollees fell into this category. Although many of these long-term enrollees would have left the program during the year, most sponsors faced the prospect of having to terminate significant numbers as of October 1, 1979, unless these enrollees could be absorbed by the PSE employer or placed in other unsubsidized jobs before that time. In some instances, particularly where unemployment rates were low or where sponsors already had fixed terms for PSE enrollees, the transition problem was minimized.

The act permits the Secretary of Labor to waive restrictions on tenure in cases of unusual hardship. An area can qualify for a waiver if its unemployment rate is 7 percent or more and if the sponsor can demonstrate that he has had unusual difficulty in placing PSE participants in unsubsidized employment. Waivers are granted only for a stipulated period of less than 12 months to afford additional time to place enrollees (*Federal Register*, 1979b, pp. 46760-46762).[12] At the time of the survey, 9 of 28 sponsors expected to apply for waivers for all or some of their participants. Others had not applied because their unemployment rates were too low, because they were informally advised by DOL staff that they would not qualify, or because they were discouraged by the cumbersome DOL waiver procedures.

The Employment and Training Administration estimated that between 200,000 and 250,000 participants reached the 18-month tenure limit as of October 1. Waiver requests were screened in regional offices, and requests for approximately 53,000 participants were forwarded to the national office; nearly all were approved. The number of waivers granted, at least in the first year, was not so high as to vitiate the congressional intent.

One of the intended effects of the tenure requirement—the stimulation of placement efforts—was being realized. Most of the sponsors in the sample were intensifying efforts to assist enrollees who would be dropped from the program. PSE employers were urged to absorb some of the participants, and job-search counseling or training was offered for enrollees about to be discharged. In New York City, where 14,000 of 26,000 enrollees were faced with termination, the city planned to seek waivers for 9,000, absorb 3,000 into regular jobs, and lay off the remaining 2,000. In a small area, Pasco County, Florida, PSE employers were urged to absorb enrollees, and participants were required to report to the employment service at least once a month for assistance in job placement. Several sponsors staggered the phaseout of enrollees to avoid a sudden, mass layoff. Cleveland, for example, terminated 300 in March and 700 more by September. The Capital Consortium (Austin) attempted to meet the problem by dropping projects as they expired. The fact that enrollment levels were expected to be lower in fiscal 1980 was an added incentive to thin out the ranks.

LONG-TERM PROBLEMS IN ADMINISTERING PSE PROGRAMS

Before reauthorization, public service programs in Titles II and VI had been simpler to administer than the comprehensive programs in other CETA titles, because the comprehensive programs involved a wider range of manpower and supportive services. But this is beginning to change. The reauthorization act, particularly Title IID, provides for supplementary remedial services including plans for developing the employability of

TABLE 3   Long-Term Problems in Administering CETA Public Service
Employment Programs, Sample Prime Sponsor Areas

	Percent of Areas	
Activity	Identify Activity as Problem	Consider Problem Most Serious[a]
Arranging for PSE positions within wage limits	57	29
Tracking length of stay of enrollees	46	11
Training and employability development	36	11
Procedures for determining and verifying eligibility	29	0
Establishing monitoring and complaint processes	21	4
Recruiting applicants under new eligibility criteria	14	11
Adjusting to uncertainties in funding	14	7
Other management problems—staffing, administrative cost limits, record keeping, etc.	32	14

Source: Based on reports from 28 areas.

[a]Some respondents noted more than one problem as most serious.

enrollees and training for those who need it. Furthermore, wage,
eligibility, and tenure restrictions—all of which are related to national
goals—increase the complexity of PSE programs. Prime sponsors report
that the "new" CETA presents a formidable array of operational and
administrative challenges (Table 3) extending beyond the transition phase.

By far the most serious difficulty is arranging for PSE positions that
meet wage restrictions and also conform to local prevailing wage
structures for entry positions. The problem will be particularly acute in
areas where wages in the public sector are high (see Chapter 4).

Establishing and maintaining systems to record the length of time that
individuals are enrolled in the program was considered a challenge by
about half of the sponsors, even those with computer systems. New York
City estimated that it would take a year to perfect a unified tracking
system for the tens of thousands of enrollees in PSE and other CETA
programs.

Arrangements for employability development and the training of PSE
workers also will be troublesome, particularly for small communities
where facilities are not available and for employers not equipped to
provide training. Many sponsors do not fully understand how to combine
training programs with PSE. Because 10 percent of the sponsor's 1979
PSE allotment must be reserved for training, sponsors felt pressed to find

approaches, but little had been accomplished in developing training strategies during the first year.

Although determining and verifying eligibility were not considered the most serious problems, nearly one-third of the sponsors expected that these time-consuming activities would continue to pose difficulties. The amount of documentation required of PSE applicants to support their eligibility is so great that some applicants, although eligible, are discouraged from applying. Several areas with low unemployment reported difficulty in recruiting workers with appropriate skills from a reduced pool of eligibles. The reauthorization generated other management chores, such as reinforcing monitoring capabilities, maintaining additional records, and supervising more closely the eligibility determination and wages paid by subcontractors, all of which add significantly to the administrative workload.

Staff Size

The greater complexity of the new CETA resulted in moderate increases in overhead staff despite declining funds (Table 4). Two-thirds of the reporting sponsors in the study group indicated that administrative staffs (excluding personnel performing direct operations such as intake of enrollees or job development and placement) had increased between 1978 and 1979. Additions were largely in the administration of public service employment programs where allowable administrative costs were cut from 15 to 10 percent. Between the two years, the average increase in administrative staff size for the local sponsors who provided data was 9 percent. Further small increases were projected for fiscal 1980, but these projections were made before cuts in allotments were announced. The administrative staff for balance of states showed similar gains.

About two-thirds of the sponsors reported that a portion of their staff was engaged in providing direct services; other sponsors either contracted out all service activities or did not provide data. Of the local prime sponsors reporting, additions in operating personnel averaged 4 percent. The major gains were in staff assigned to job development and placement activities, reflecting the emphasis on placement activities in the reauthorization act.

In general, the heavier administrative load has not significantly affected the size of staff or the CETA organization of govermental units below the prime sponsor level. There were some exceptions: In the balance of Texas, for example, where central office staff has been reduced, the burden of the new reauthorization requirements has been passed on to councils of government. Counties in Maine are developing capabilities for monitoring,

TABLE 4   Average Size of Staff, Sample Local Prime Sponsor Areas, Fiscal 1978-1979

	Fiscal 1978	Fiscal 1979	Percent Change 1978-79
	Administrative Staff		
TOTAL	42.1	46.0	+ 9.3
Planning	5.6	5.8	+ 3.6
Monitoring/Evaluation	7.6	8.4	+10.5
Administrative Support	14.5	17.9	+23.4
Other	14.5	13.9	- 4.1
	Operating Staff		
TOTAL	33.6	34.9	+ 3.9

Source: Based on reports from 20 areas (administrative staff) and 17 areas (operating staff). Excludes balance of states.

NOTE: Details may not add to totals due to rounding.

preparing employability development plans, and transition of enrollees. The city of Lansing, a program agent under the Lansing Tri-County Regional Manpower Consortium, set up its own system for processing applicants and verifying eligibility. The rural contractor in the Capital Consortium of Texas has arranged for monitoring and eligibility verification.

Use of Subcontractors

Other measures of administrative activity are the number and the kinds of organizations that provide PSE jobs. In the local study areas for which data were supplied, the average number of employing units declined 7 percent between 1978 and 1979, reflecting the drop in expenditures and enrollments. Of 13 sponsors reporting declines in the number of employers, 6 attributed them to smaller budgets. Only 2 sponsors attributed these declines to wage or other programmatic restrictions in the 1978 amendments.

Although some shifts were noted in the proportion of PSE contractors that were government agencies as compared with private nonprofit employers in individual areas, overall there was almost no change (Table 5). The greater use of nonprofit agencies in some areas was most frequently attributed to the wage restrictions, which nonprofit organizations are more able to accommodate. Areas reporting greater use of government agencies

TABLE 5   Average Number and Type of CETA Public Service Employment Program Employing Units, Sample Local Prime Sponsor Areas, Fiscal 1978-1979

Type of Employer	Fiscal 1978		Fiscal 1979	
	Number	Percent	Number	Percent
TOTAL	104	100	97	100
Government	57	55	52	54
Nonprofit	47	45	44	46

Source: Based on reports from 22 areas. Excludes balance of states.

NOTE: Details may not add to totals due to rounding.

observed that nonprofit organizations are less able to provide training mandated by the legislation and that supervision of such agencies is more difficult.

Administrative Costs

Despite a decrease in the number of employing agencies, the ratio of administrative costs to total expenditures is increasing. Congress cut the proportion of funds available for administration of public service employment programs from 15 percent of allotted funds in 1978 to 10 percent in 1979, and required that an additional 10 percent of funds was to be reserved for training.[13] The lowering of administrative costs to 10 percent in fiscal 1979, combined with an overall decrease in allotments, hampered administration or operations in nearly half of the cases, according to CETA administrators and program agents interviewed. Sponsors who shared costs with project operators were particularly squeezed. The most common complaint was that the lower limit tended to reduce staff at a time when administrative tasks were increasing. For example, as a result of the wage restrictions, Philadelphia has had to use many more nonprofit organizations as PSE employers; this shift is expected to entail more supervision and administrative support.

Survey data show that, despite the cut in the allowable percentage, administrative cost ratios were higher in the first six months of 1979 than in 1978. For the United States as a whole, administrative costs were 8.4 percent of expenditures under Title II and 8.9 percent of expenditures under Title VI during the first six months of fiscal 1979. Although these figures are significantly higher than the respective figures of 6.5 and 7.3 percent for 1978, they are well below the 10 percent limit. Beginning in

36 THE NEW CETA

April, sponsors were permitted to commingle administrative funds for all titles—a change that increases flexibility but that makes cost analysis more difficult.

COORDINATION WITH OTHER PROGRAMS AND AGENCIES

INTEGRATING PSE WITH CETA TRAINING ACTIVITIES

With its increased emphasis on serving the structurally unemployed, PSE was brought closer to other CETA programs that focused more directly on improving the employability of persons with labor market handicaps. In fiscal 1978, expenditures for training and supportive services for PSE participants were negligible for two reasons: (1) training funds came out of the administrative cost account and (2) in the haste to increase PSE enrollments during the 1977-1978 buildup, there was little time for designing supplemental training programs.

To underscore the intent that public service employment programs for the structurally unemployed enhance employability, the new legislation grouped Title IID with the other employability development programs under Title II of the act. Congress also required that 10 percent of allotted funds be reserved for training, and called for employability development plans for each Title IID participant.[14]

Half of the sponsors interviewed reported closer links between Title IID and Title IIB (employability development programs) at least in the planning stage. Nearly all of the sponsors who reported closer coordination plan either to move Title IIB trainees into Title IID jobs for further work experience or to arrange some classroom training for Title IID participants. The plans of other sponsors include more counseling or remedial education for Title IID participants, and in a handful of cases child care or transportation services. Although it is too early to arrive at a definite finding, the shift toward a more disadvantaged population and the attempt to provide some employability services point to a more client-oriented approach in the public service jobs programs.

COORDINATION WITH OTHER AGENCIES

Coordination of CETA with activities of other community agencies in joint activities using CETA labor was widespread among the survey areas. Nearly all sponsors have programs in which CETA enrollees participate in weatherization or housing rehabilitation projects for low-income and elderly persons. CETA provides labor while the Commmunity Services Administration or other agencies supply funds for the materials. Projects of this kind are difficult to arrange because they involve meshing activities of agencies with different regulations and time schedules. Most of these joint activities were initiated before the reauthorization act, and due to the limits on the duration of CETA projects, some are being phased out. The reduction in PSE funds and limitation on wages may further curtail these projects despite the emphasis on coordination in the act and in DOL regulations.[15]

CETA/EMPLOYMENT SERVICE RELATIONS

The Comprehensive Employment and Training Act of 1973 established a national employment and training system and placed it under the jurisdiction of state and local governments. Control over the local programs was placed in the hands of local elected officials. Under this decentralized design there were no designated deliverers of employment and training services. Selection of organizations to implement CETA programs was left to the prime sponsors, taking into consideration demonstrated effectiveness.

The effect of this policy was to undercut the primary role that the employment service (ES) enjoyed as the presumptive deliverer of services such as selection of enrollees and job placement under the Manpower Development and Training Act and other pre-CETA manpower programs. By 1976, in ES offices, the number of positions supported by manpower training funds (other than the Work Incentive (WIN) program) had declined by more than one-third from fiscal 1974, but these losses were offset by an increased number of ES positions to aid in administering public service employment programs.

The passage of the Emergency Jobs Programs Extension Act of 1976 and the expansion of PSE under the economic stimulus program further enhanced the employment service role. To facilitate the speedy expansion of PSE, the Employment and Training Administration urged prime sponsors to use employment service offices for establishing pools of potentially eligible applicants and for certifying the eligibility of applicants. As inducements to both parties, prime sponsors who used the employment service were excused from liability for ineligible enrollees, and employment service offices were given budget credits for referrals to CETA PSE positions. The incentives worked. Nearly all sponsors entered into or continued existing agreements with employment service offices, and PSE placements became a sizeable proportion of all employment service placements. Moreover the experience of working together helped to improve relationships between the two major manpower systems (National Research Council, 1980, pp. 67-72, 83-86).

TABLE 6   Changes in Employment Service Role in CETA Public Service
Employment Activities, Sample Prime Sponsor Areas, Fiscal 1978-1980

Activity	Percent of Sponsors Utilizing Employment Service		
	FY 1978	FY 1979	FY 1980
Labor market information	89	89	81
Advance listing of PSE openings for notification of veterans	78	78	67
Recruitment activities	85	81	74
Maintenance of applicant pool	81	67	59
Applicant screening, interviewing, and eligibility determination	89	78	63
Eligibility verification	70	59	44
Referral to CETA administration	56	56	56
Referral to hiring agencies	52	44	37
Job development	59	56	59
Placement of terminees	78	78	74

Source: Based on reports from 27 areas.

The reauthorization act did not directly address the issue of ES-CETA
relationships.[16] However, revised DOL regulations for the first time
mandated a formal agreement between each prime sponsor and the state
employment security agency. In other respects the act tends to weaken the
ties between the two systems. Most importantly, the assignment of liability
to the prime sponsor for ineligible enrollments has removed a key incentive
for cooperation. To protect themselves, sponsors are increasingly performing the verification function rather than delegating it to the ES or other
agencies (Table 6). After the PSE expansion goals were reached, use of ES
for maintaining a pool of applicants decreased. As a consequence, the role
of the employment service may be receding from the high point reached
during the enrollment buildup prior to the reauthorization. Most sponsors
continue to rely on ES offices for labor market information, for recruiting
of applicants for public service employment positions, and for placement
of those leaving the program.

Twenty-three of the twenty-eight prime sponsors in the NRC study
indicated that the ES role in CETA had changed; about half of the changes
were attributed to the reauthorization act. In Philadelphia, a private
organization took over the Title IID intake functions formerly performed
by the employment service. The Lansing consortium did not renew an ES
contract for recruitment, screening, or eligibility verification mainly

because of the liability provisions. A number of areas discontinued using the employment service for applicant pools.

On the other hand, several sponsors reported enlarging the role of the employment service as a result of reauthorization provisions. In Middlesex County, for example, the employment service was enlisted to help with desk audits for eligibility determination, job-search assistance for enrollees, and expanded job development and placement. Stanislaus County, faced with the large number of enrollees who were being terminated at the same time, turned to the employment service for more job development assistance; and in the Pinellas–St. Petersburg consortium, the employment service was assigned responsibility for Title VI employability development plans. Overall, however, the employment service is playing a smaller role in public service employment activities than it did in the past. The decline is reflected in a sharp drop in the number of referrals to CETA programs by the employment service between fiscal 1978 and fiscal 1979 (Table 7). CETA currently accounts for 20 percent of employment service placements compared with 25 percent in the previous year, due to fewer new enrollments in CETA as well as to reduced use of ES services.

Several sponsors reported changes in the employment service role that were not related to the CETA reauthorization: Lorain County, which has withdrawn its contract with the employment service for intake and certification; and the balance of Maine, where a number of counties are switching from the employment service to community-based organizations for a variety of activities.

In two-thirds of the survey areas, relationships with the employment service were reported to be satisfactory. Some improvements were noted as relationships have stabilized over the years. In the remaining survey areas, there were lingering problems in CETA-ES relationships, but the complaints were not new. Historical rivalries, turf problems, competition for placements, lack of commitment, and "too much bureaucracy" were among the problems cited by CETA personnel. These problems have been exacerbated as more pressure has been placed on prime sponsors for program results.

EFFECT OF CETA REAUTHORIZATION ON FEDERAL-LOCAL
RELATIONS

The delineation of federal and local roles in the CETA program has been unclear and controversial. The original concept of a decategorized and decentralized block grant system implied considerable local latitude within a broad framework of federal policy and accountability. But the amendments to CETA since 1973 have narrowed the span of local control.

TABLE 7   Individuals Placed by the Employment Service and Placements in
CETA, Fiscal 1976–1979 (thousands)

		ES Placements in CETA			
Fiscal Year	Total Individuals Placed by ES	Total	On-the-Job Training	Public Service Employment	Work Experience
		Number of Individuals			
1976[a]	3,367	388	38	201	149
1977	4,138	772	54	334	384
1978	4,623	1,108	63	579	466
1979[b]	4,537	849	48	393	408
		Percent of Total			
1976	100	11	1	6	4
1977	100	18	1	8	9
1978	100	25	1	13	10
1979	100	20	1	9	9

Source: Employment and Training Administration, U.S. Department of Labor (unpublished data).

[a]July 1975–June 1976.
[b]Preliminary.

NOTE: Details may not add to totals due to rounding.

Local choice has been reduced by the enactment of new categorical programs to address special problems and by the considerable number of prescriptions to bring local programs into closer alignment with national policies.

The addition of public service employment programs, new youth programs, and, more recently, private sector initiatives has limited the range of CETA activities.[17] Although sponsors exercise some flexibility in resource allocations within the allotments for each separate title and subtitle, they generally feel that local initiative has been restricted. The freedom of local officials has been even more limited by federal specifications for choosing clients, setting wage levels, and determining duration of employment.

The effect of the CETA reauthorization on relationships between federal and local officials was perceived differently by CETA sponsors and DOL regional office personnel. CETA administrators tended to believe that the reauthorization act resulted in more federal intervention in local affairs, more detailed supervision, and more compliance activity. In contrast, most regional office personnel did not think that the amendments had a significant effect on DOL relationships with prime sponsors, but several acknowledged a stronger role since the act was passed.

Federal activities, particularly review of plans and monitoring, were increased as a result of the reauthorization. A number of sponsors thought that the federal government provided more technical assistance, but the assistance tended to be in procedural matters and regulations rather than in substantive program areas, such as establishing models for combining training with PSE.

Two-thirds of the sponsors in the study group reported serious differences with regional office personnel since reauthorization. Most frequently, these concerned federal pressure for stepped-up enrollments and expenditures. Other differences related to transition plans, establishment of independent monitoring units, conversion of PSE jobs under the new wage structure, adjustment in intake systems to accommodate the new eligibility determination procedures, and frequency of reporting.

A significant proportion of prime sponsors (10 of 28) complained of confusing interpretations of rules, delays in answering queries, and lack of responsiveness. These complaints reflected the general instability in program direction during the transition period. Several respondents noted that regional officials had similar complaints since most decisions had to be made in Washington. In the view of these respondents, the problem resulted less from the actions of regional personnel than from the actions of Congress and the Department of Labor. The specificity of the act, crafted to keep the program on its prescribed track, diminishes the flexibility of the Department of Labor as well as that of local sponsors.

SUMMARY

The administration of CETA has been made more difficult by several features of the reauthorization act, particularly the redesign of public service employment programs and the introduction of new programs. Moreover, changes in the planning system and increased monitoring and compliance activity, and particularly the shifts and uncertainties in funding, have placed additional stress on the system.

• The new planning requirements, intended to reduce paperwork, have increased the amount of detail that plans must include. Most of the CETA administrators and planners interviewed felt that the new planning documents were as difficult and time-consuming as past plans. Although plans may be better structured than in the past and more useful for identifying target groups, it is questionable whether they are more useful for other operations and evaluation.

• The mandated broadening of membership on planning councils has not affected their influence. The local decision-making process has remained the same, with PSE decisions usually made by CETA staff in consultation with elected officials or with planning councils.

• Far-reaching changes in public service employment program policy and regulations, combined with shifts in funding, contributed to administrative instability in many areas during 1979. Although organizational structures were usually not affected, operations were in an almost constant state of flux. Confusion about rules for eligibility and wages, repeated modification of grants, changes in enrollment goals, and rigid termination deadlines for enrollees were among the problems faced by sponsors.

• The activities that are expected to cause the most serious long-term problems are anticipated in administering the wage provisions, tracking the length of stay of participants, and providing training and employability development. About one-third of the sponsors anticipate difficulty in implementing the eligibility determination and verification procedures.

• The cumulative effect of changes in the act has been to increase record-keeping and reporting, as well as planning and monitoring activities. The size of administrative and operational staffs is increasing. Administrative cost ratios for PSE are rising as the programs become more complex.

• Despite pressure from the Employment and Training Administration, the role of the employment service in CETA public service employment programs has diminished. When liability for ineligible participants was assigned to prime sponsors, a major incentive for using the employment service was eliminated.

• Relationships between local sponsors and the federal establishment are also changing; federal intervention has increased and more emphasis has been placed on compliance activities, according to CETA administrators. The new stipulations go far in the direction of recategorizing and recentralizing CETA. Funds are channeled into particular programs and a maze of specific rules restricts administrative discretion.

NOTES

1. The FY 1980 appropriation for Titles IID and VI, enacted on October 12, 1979, amounted to $3,112 million, only 71 percent of the administration's budget request. The fiscal 1980 planning estimates for Titles IID and VI, issued on May 15, totaled $3,701 million; allocations announced on October 2, including reallocated carry-in funds and discretionary funds, came to $3,436 million.

Variations between the May and October figures were much wider for individual sponsors.

2. Data refer to councils other than balance of states.

3. By the end of fiscal 1979, 400 of 470 prime sponsors had set up PICs and an additional 20 were being formed.

4. Cities and counties with a population of 50,000 or more are "program agents" under the act. They operate public service employment programs in their jurisdictions with supervision from prime sponsors. In balance of states, some measure of program planning or administration is often delegated to other subjurisdictions—councils of government, counties, or other government or nongovernment agencies.

5. The Raleigh consortium broke up on October 1, 1979. The city, itself, became a prime sponsor and the three counties joined the "balance of state."

6. The act has a total of eight sets of eligibility requirements for various subparts. In addition to criteria for Titles IID and VI, special rules apply to Title IIB, Title IIC upgrading, Title IIC retraining, and to three youth program components. These involve determinations of family income, prior unemployment or employment, age, residence, educational status, etc. See pp. VI-23 to VI-26 in the U.S. Department of Labor (1979a) *Forms Preparation Handbook*.

7. ETA Field Memorandum No. 39-79, October 31, 1978. Because of quarterly reporting, DOL was not aware at that time that enrollments had declined. In response to the need for more timely information, the Office of Management and Budget later authorized semimonthly enrollment reports.

8. Under the reauthorization act, equal weight is given to four factors in the Title IID formula: the total number of unemployed in each area; the number of unemployed in excess of a 4.5 percent unemployment rate; the number of unemployed in areas of substantial unemployment; and the number of adults in low-income families. Previously, Title II funds were distributed on the basis of only one factor—the relative number of unemployed in areas of substantial unemployment. The basis for identifying areas of substantial unemployment was also changed in fiscal 1980 from an unemployment rate of 6.5 percent for 3 consecutive months to an average of 6.5 percent for the most recent 12 months. The Title VI formula was not changed.

9. Because Title IID or Title VI funds were being underutilized, the Employment and Training Administration withdrew Title IID and Title VI funds from 49 sponsors for reallocation to other sponsors who had been determined to be able to use more funds effectively. In addition, 25 of the sponsors returned excess 1979 funds. In making the fiscal 1980 allocations, all unspent funds in excess of 10 percent of each prime sponsor's fiscal 1979 Title IID and Title VI allotments were pooled and reallocated.

10. In December 1979, PSE enrollments totaled 395,000, significantly below the 450,000 level projected for fiscal 1980.

11. The report notes, however, that data are obtained from prime sponsor records, which may not reflect precisely the date on which enrollees stopped receiving services.

12. The waiver request must include a detailed transition plan for four quarters or less. Under very exceptional circumstances, a subsequent waiver may be granted.

13. In fiscal 1980 and thereafter, the 10 percent administrative cost limit is retained for Title IID, but is increased to 15 percent for Title VI.

14. See statements by Senators Gaylord Nelson and Jacob Javits, *Congressional Record* (1978b), pp. 13953, 13955, and 13968. See also U.S. Congress (1978b), pp. 29-30.

15. An interagency agreement between the Department of Energy and the Department of Labor, approved September 1979, calls for joint efforts to increase the level of CETA support for weatherization projects.

16. Section 5(a) requires the Secretary of Labor to recommend improvements in the Wagner-Peyser Act to ensure coordination with CETA, but the DOL has not yet filed its report.

17. It is noted, however, that the amount of funds appropriated for comprehensive manpower programs under Title I (Title II A, B, and C), which is relatively less restricted, has increased from $1,580 million in FY 1975 to $2,054 million in FY 1980 (see Appendix A, Table A- 1).

3 Participants

The reauthorization act has had a sudden and sharp impact on the characteristics profile of new public service employment (PSE) enrollees. Those groups that have traditionally been thought to face disadvantages in the labor market—women, youth, blacks, and persons from low-income families—obtained a much larger proportion of PSE jobs in fiscal 1979 than they had in fiscal 1978. Persons better able to compete in the labor market—individuals with post–high school education and unemployment insurance claimants, who by definition have had some work experience—participated less frequently in fiscal 1979.

However, other groups that were of particular concern to Congress—recipients of Aid to Families with Dependent Children (AFDC), Vietnam-era veterans, and disabled veterans—did not benefit from the reauthorization act. The proportion of these groups enrolled in the PSE programs showed little change from the previous year.

The act has succeeded in converting Title II into a PSE program for the structurally unemployed. However, in terms of client characteristics, the objective of establishing separate Title IID and VI programs that serve distinctly different clienteles has not been achieved. The characteristics of new enrollees suggest that there is little difference between the needs of persons currently enrolled in these two programs.

45

DETERMINING WHOM TO SERVE

Early efforts to direct PSE jobs to specific segments of the unemployed population took two forms: eligibility requirements and targeting directives. The eligibility requirements set the minimum criteria for participation in the PSE programs, while the targeting directives identified the groups in the eligible population that Congress expected the PSE programs to serve. This arrangement was intended to ensure that national objectives would be realized while allowing some flexibility at the local level so that community needs could be met. In practice, however, national targeting objectives tended to be subordinated to the local desire to select the best qualified applicants for PSE positions.

The principal shortcoming of these early provisions was that they did not sufficiently restrict access to the PSE programs. During fiscal 1975, approximately 387,000 persons participated in PSE programs. These participants were selected from an eligible population of over 18 million. Thus, there were approximately 48 persons eligible for each PSE opening. Under these conditions, targeting was left to local officials who, not surprisingly, acted much like private sector employers and usually sought to select the best-qualified applicants available.

Dissatisfaction with the results of this selection pattern was manifested in the Emergency Jobs Programs Extension Act of 1976 (EJPEA). Congress and the administration were concerned not only that the most disadvantaged were not adequately represented in PSE jobs but that the hiring of skilled, job-ready applicants for PSE positions increased the probability that PSE employees would be used to perform tasks that ordinarily would be funded by local revenues.

The tightened EJPEA eligibility requirements reduced the size of the population eligible for the majority of Title VI positions from 19 million to 4 million and significantly increased the proportion of severely disadvantaged persons in the eligible population.[1] This limited the discretion exercised by local officials in selecting participants for this part of the PSE program.

In terms of the whole PSE program, however, EJPEA did not have as large an impact on the characteristics of participants as Congress had anticipated. Although the new eligibility requirements reduced the size of the population eligible for many Title VI positions, there were still 15 persons eligible for each of these PSE jobs. In addition, many of the effects of the tighter Title VI provisions were offset by the hiring for Title II positions and those Title VI positions that were subject to looser entry requirements. Finally, although EJPEA established guidelines that identified the groups Congress expected to be served, they, like their predecessors, were ineffective because they encompassed too many groups, were not binding, and were not perceived by local officials as being relevant to their programs.

REAUTHORIZATION ACT PROVISIONS

The eligibility requirements, wage restrictions, and targeting guidelines of the reauthorization act of 1978 represented another attempt to direct PSE jobs to the disadvantaged. While EJPEA had moved the PSE programs in this direction, the consensus at the federal level was that it had not gone far enough.

There were other reasons for focusing PSE on the disadvantaged. Congress and the administration, concerned with rising inflation, did not want to constrict the supply of skilled, job-ready workers by enrolling them in PSE jobs. It was also believed that an increased emphasis in PSE on enhancing the skills of the structurally unemployed would yield future dividends in the form of a more productive labor force. Finally, focusing PSE on the disadvantaged was viewed by some as a test of the feasibility of using CETA as a vehicle for welfare reform.

The reauthorization act was also expected to establish separate PSE programs serving the structurally and cyclically unemployed. The distinction between Titles II and VI had become increasingly muddled in the years preceding the reauthorization act. The original difference between these two titles was described by Senator Gaylord Nelson in the report of the Senate Committee on Labor and Public Welfare: Title II " . . . was designed to deal with the kind of chronic, high unemployment that persists in some areas in good and bad times; . . . Title VI, however, was countercyclical in purpose and intended to combat the severe unemployment that became pervasive throughout the Nation as a result of the recession" (U.S. Congress 1976b, p. 16). When EJPEA tightened the eligibility requirements for the majority of Title VI positions without tightening the requirements for Title II, it created the anomalous situation in which the eligibility requirements for the cyclically unemployed were much stricter than the requirement for the structurally unemployed. One of the purposes of the reauthorization act was to reestablish a two-part PSE program that would provide services to increase the employability of the structurally unemployed in Title IID.

The reauthorization act contains four basic categories of provisions that affect the selection of PSE participants: eligibility requirements, eligibility determination and verification procedures, targeting guidelines, and wage restrictions (see chart, p. 48-49).

CETA—Changes in Eligibility and Targeting for Public Service Employment, 1973-1978

Date	Act	Title	Eligibility	Targeting
Dec. 28, 1973	Comprehensive Employment and Training Act of 1973 PL 93-203	II Areas of Substantial Unemployment	1. Unemployed 30 days or more or underemployed.	1. Consideration for most severely disadvantaged in terms of length of unemployment and prospects of obtaining a job; Vietnam veterans; and former manpower trainees. Equitable treatment for significant segments of the unemployed population.
Dec. 31, 1974	Emergency Jobs and Unemployment Assistance Act of 1974 PL 93-567	VI Countercyclical public service employment	2. Unemployed 30 days or more or underemployed. For areas of excessively high unemployment (7 percent or more), unemployed 15 instead of 30 days.	2. The same as in 1, above. Also preferred consideration for: the unemployed who have exhausted UI benefits; unemployed not eligible for UI (except new entrants); persons unemployed 15 or more weeks; recently separated veterans (within last 4 years).
Oct. 1, 1976	Emergency Jobs Programs Extension Act of 1976 PL 94-444	VI Countercyclical public service employment	3. *For half of vacancies in regular positions above June 1976 level:* the same as in 2, above.	3. *For half of vacancies in regular positions above June 1976 levels:* the same as in 2, above.
			4. *For the remaining half of regular vacancies and for new project positions:* (a) member of low-income family, and (b) either received unemployment insurance for 15 or more weeks, was not eligible for UI	4. *For the remaining half of regular vacancies and for new project positions:* the same as in 2, above. In addition, equitable allocation of jobs among: members of low-income families who received unemployment insurance for 15 or more weeks, were not eligible

| Oct. 27, 1978 | Comprehensive Employment and Training Act Amendments of 1978 PL 95-524 | IID Public service employment for the economically disadvantaged | 5. Unemployed 15 weeks, unemployed at time of determination, and member of low-income family; or member of family receiving AFDC or SSI. (Low-income defined as family income of less than 70 percent of the BLS lower living standard or the OMB poverty level.) | 5. Intended for most severely disadvantaged in terms of length of unemployment and prospects of obtaining a job. Consideration to be given to: Vietnam-era veterans; public assistance recipients; groups facing labor market disadvantages, identified as: offenders, persons of limited English language proficiency, handicapped, women, single parents, displaced homemakers, youth, older workers, persons lacking educational credentials, and others named by the Secretary of Labor. Equitable treatment for significant segments of the unemployed population. |
| | | VI Countercyclical public service employment | 6. Unemployed 10 of last 12 weeks, and unemployed at time of determination; and an AFDC or SSI recipient or a member of a low-income family. (Low-income is defined as a family income of less than 100 percent of the BLS lower living standard.) | 6. The same as in 5, above. |

but was unemployed for 15 or more weeks, exhausted UI entitlement, or was an AFDC recipient. (Low-income defined as family income of less than 70 percent of the BLS lower level family budget.)

for UI but were unemployed 15 or more weeks, exhausted UI entitlement, or were AFDC recipients. (Low-income defined as family income of less than 70 percent of the BLS lower level family budget.)

49

ELIGIBILITY REQUIREMENTS

The eligibility requirements of the reauthorization act, as implemented by the Department of Labor (DOL), identify two populations eligible for PSE, one for Title IID and one for Title VI. However, as discussed later in the chapter, these populations are in fact quite similar. To be eligible for Title IID, a person must meet the following criteria:

• be economically disadvantaged[2] and unemployed at the time of application and for 15 of the 20 weeks immediately prior to application or
• be a member of a family that is receiving public assistance;
• reside within the prime sponsor's jurisdiction subject to certain exceptions; and
• not have voluntarily terminated his or her last full-time employment, without good cause, within the six months immediately prior to application.

These Title IID eligibility requirements are much tighter than those previously in effect for Title II and are basically the same as those that were applicable to Title VI projects in fiscal 1978.

The reauthorization act Title VI entry requirements are only a little looser than those for Title IID with respect to duration of unemployment and family income. The provisions affecting residency, voluntary termination of employment, and unemployment status prior to application for enrollment are the same (*Federal Register*, 1979a, p. 20001). With respect to duration of unemployment and family income, an individual must meet the following criteria for eligibility under Title VI:

• be unemployed for at least 10 of the 12 weeks immediately prior to application; and
• be a member of a family with an income not exceeding 100 percent of the Bureau of Labor Statistics' lower living standard based on annualization of that family's income for the three months prior to application for PSE employment or
• be a member of a family that has been receiving public assistance for 10 of the 12 weeks immediately prior to application.

The new eligibility requirements for Title VI are considerably more stringent than the fiscal 1978 requirements for Title II and the nonproject portion of Title VI. However, both the required length of unemployment and the required level of family income are less restrictive than the criteria for Title VI project positions in the preauthorization period. The net effect of these changes on participant characteristics is examined in the latter part of this chapter.

DETERMINING ELIGIBILITY

Because a significant proportion of ineligible participants (between 10 and 25 percent) were hired during the PSE enrollment buildup of fiscal 1977-1978 (National Research Council, 1980, p. 110), Congress, in the reauthorization act, took steps to ensure that only eligible persons would be enrolled in PSE programs. Prime sponsors are now required to follow highly specific procedures in determining and verifying eligibility. In addition, Congress specified that prime sponsors were to be held financially liable for ineligible participants in the event that the procedures were not followed. The subjects of eligibility verification and liability are dealt with at greater length in Chapter 6.

TARGETING GUIDELINES

In an attempt to accommodate various constituents, Congress set targeting guidelines that identified at least 17 groups that are to receive preference in the participant selection process. The reauthorization act also required that prime sponsors allocate jobs equitably among specified segments of the eligible population. The complexity of the task is best illustrated by examining the actual language of the act. Consider the following:

- PSE under this act is intended for eligible persons who are *the most severely disadvantaged* in terms of their length of unemployment and their prospects for finding employment.
- Special consideration in filling public service jobs shall be given to eligible *disabled and Vietnam-era veterans*, eligible persons who are *public assistance recipients*, and *persons who are eligible for public assistance* but not receiving such assistance.
- Special emphasis in filling public service jobs shall be given to *persons who face particular disadvantages* in specific and general labor markets or occupations, including *offenders, persons of limited English language proficiency, handicapped individuals, women, single parents, displaced homemakers, youth, older workers, individuals who lack educational credentials, public assistance recipients, and other persons* who the secretary determines require special assistance.
- Employment and training opportunities for participants shall be made available by prime sponsors on an equitable basis in accordance with the purposes of this act among *significant segments (age, sex, race, and*

national origin) of the eligible population giving consideration to the relative numbers of eligible persons in each segment (U.S. Congress, 1978d, Sect. 122(b)(1)(A)).

The inclusion of so many target groups obscures rather than clarifies the intentions of Congress; if everyone in the eligible population is a member of a target group, there can be no effective targeting.

WAGE RESTRICTIONS

The most innovative and controversial of the reauthorization act provisions are the wage restrictions. These placed constraints on the average wage that can be paid for PSE jobs and on the supplementation of PSE wages with non-CETA funds. The specific wage provisions are detailed in Chapter 4.

The authors of the reauthorization act anticipated that the wage restrictions would affect the characteristics profile of the PSE clientele in several ways. First, the lower wage might make PSE jobs less attractive to skilled, job-ready applicants, leaving PSE positions for those with the fewest employment alternatives. Second, because of the wage restrictions and the requirement that PSE participants be paid at the rate prevailing for comparable work, sponsors might find it necessary to restructure PSE programs and exclude some high-wage occupations. As a result, PSE positions would require less skill and would therefore be more accessible to those most in need of assistance. Finally, the different wage supplementation provisions in Titles IID and VI might help to distinguish the clienteles served by these programs. The elimination of wage supplementation in Title IID might result in the selection of a greater proportion of structurally unemployed individuals.

CHARACTERISTICS OF NEW ENROLLEES

CHANGES FROM FISCAL 1978 TO FISCAL 1979

The reauthorization act appears to have produced a swift and substantial shift in the characteristics profile of new enrollees. Overall, the changes are leading in the direction Congress intended. The increases in PSE participation registered by blacks, women, and economically disadvantaged individuals are quite pronounced. School age youth and persons with less than 12 years of education have made more limited gains. Other groups have not fared as well, however. Vietnam-era and disabled veterans and AFDC recipients—target groups given special emphasis in the reauthorization act—have yet to benefit. While changes in the profile of new enrollees were evident in both PSE programs, they were much more pronounced in Title IID, particularly in the proportions of black and economically disadvantaged enrollees.

In general, the changes in participant characteristics were larger in the second half of fiscal 1979, the period in which the reauthorization act requirements became fully effective. The timing of these changes will be considered further in the third section of this chapter, which explores the factors responsible for the changes in the characteristics of PSE participants.

Sex

The proportion of women participating in PSE rose sharply in fiscal 1979. According to the Continuous Longitudinal Manpower Survey[3] (CLMS) data (Table 8), 48 percent of participants enrolled in the second half of fiscal 1979 were women, a gain of 10 percentage points over the previous year. Women had been gaining as a proportion of PSE enrollees since fiscal 1975 (see Appendix A, Table A-2). However, during the transition period, October 1978 to March 1979, the proportion of women jumped from 38 to 45 percent. The magnitude of the increases and their timing were similar in Titles IID and VI.

Minority Status

Black participation in the PSE programs rose substantially in fiscal 1979. The proportion of black new enrollees increased from 29 percent in fiscal 1978 to 37 percent in the second half of fiscal 1979. All of this increase occurred in the second half of the fiscal year. While the increase in black participation was evident in both PSE programs, the change in Title IID was sharper than in Title VI. The magnitude of the increase in Title IID is partially accounted for by the fact that Title II had less restrictive eligibility requirements in fiscal 1978 and therefore served a lower proportion of blacks (24 percent) than Title VI (30 percent).

The level of participation of other minority groups did not change in fiscal 1979. Hispanics continued to hold about 7 percent of all new PSE jobs while the proportion of new positions filled by all other minorities, primarily native Americans, rose from 2 to 3 percent, a statistically insignificant change.[4] Titles IID and VI exhibit the same basic pattern, although the proportion of Hispanics may have declined slightly in Title VI during the second half of fiscal 1979.

TABLE 8 Selected Characteristics of Newly Enrolled Participants, Title II (IID) and Title VI, Fiscal 1978-1979

Selected Characteristics	Titles IID and VI			Title IID			Title VI		
		Fiscal 1979			Fiscal 1979			Fiscal 1979	
	Fiscal 1978	Oct. 1978-March 1979	April 1979-Sept. 1979	Fiscal 1978	Oct. 1978-March 1979	April 1979-Sept. 1979	Fiscal 1978	Oct. 1978-March 1979	April 1979-Sept. 1979
TOTAL ENROLLED	567,217	172,202	111,661	92,978	47,666	104,530	474,239	124,536	118,858
Percent Distribution									
Total	100	100	100	100	100	100	100	100	100
Sex: Male	62	55	52	58	53	49	63	55	54
Female	38	45	48	42	47	51	37	45	46
Minority Status:									
White (not Hispanic)	61	60	54	68	60	54	60	60	54
Black (not Hispanic)	29	29	37	24	28	37	30	29	37
Hispanic	7	8	6	6	10	6	8	7	5
Other	2	3	3	3	2	3	2	4	3
Age:									
19 and under	10	10	14	10	9	14	11	10	15
20-21	13	11	14	13	13	14	13	10	13
22-24	64	68	62	63	66	61	65	69	63
45-54	8	7	6	9	7	6	8	7	5
55 and over	5	4	4	6	5	4	4	3	4
Economically Disadvantaged	84	92	95	66	92	97	89	92	93
Receiving unemployment insurance at entry	13	10	9	14	9	8	13	11	9

Source: Westat, Inc., Continuous Longitudinal Manpower Survey, preliminary data (unpublished), provided by the Employment and Training Administration, U.S. Department of Labor.

NOTE: Details may not add to 100 percent due to rounding.

Age

Youth 19 years of age and under increased their share of new PSE positions in the second half of fiscal 1979 to 14 percent, an increase of 4 percentage points above the fiscal 1978 level. All of this increase, which reverses a downward trend in the participation of youth since 1975, occurred in the second half of the fiscal year and was distributed evenly in Titles IID and VI.

The increased participation of school age youth was offset by small declines in the proportion of new enrollees in the older age categories. Again, the pattern was the same in Titles IID and VI.

Economically Disadvantaged

The proportion of newly enrolled PSE participants who were economically disadvantaged at entry rose from 84 percent in fiscal 1978 to 95 percent in the second half of fiscal 1979. This shift became evident during the transition period and continued through the remainder of the fiscal year. The increase was concentrated in Title IID, where the proportion of economically disadvantaged new enrollees leaped 31 percentage points as compared to a increase of 4 points in Title VI. The magnitude of the change in Title IID reflects the fact that Title II did not have a family income eligibility requirement prior to the reauthorization act. In fiscal 1978, only 66 percent of the new enrollees in Title II were economically disadvantaged compared to 89 percent in Title VI. Title IID now enrolls a slightly higher proportion of economically disadvantaged individuals than Title VI as a result of the tightened Title IID eligibility requirements.

Unemployment Insurance Claimants

In fiscal 1976, when the unemployment insurance (UI) system was overwhelmed by vast numbers of long-term unemployed, Congress expressed interest in moving UI claimants into PSE jobs. This interest was written into the Emergency Jobs Programs Extension Act of 1976 and is evident in the high proportion of UI claimants in PSE jobs in fiscal 1977 (16 percent). As the number of insured unemployed declined from a weekly average of 4.9 million in 1975 to 2.6 million in 1978, congressional concern also declined. Unemployment insurance claimants are not a target group in the 1978 CETA reauthorization act. As a result of the 1978 act and the further decline in the number of insured unemployed, the proportion of new PSE enrollees receiving unemployment insurance at entry declined from 13 percent in fiscal 1978 to 10 percent in the first half

TABLE 9 Selected Characteristics of Participants, Title II (IID) and Title VI, Sample Prime Sponsor Areas, Fiscal 1978 and January-June 1979

Selected Characteristics	Titles IID and VI		Title IID		Title VI	
	Individuals Served Fiscal 1978	New Enrollees Jan.-June 1979[a]	Individuals Served Fiscal 1978	New Enrollees Jan.-June 1979[a]	Individuals Served Fiscal 1978	New Enrollees Jan.-June 1979[a]
TOTAL ENROLLED	36,849	7,407	6,480	4,029	30,369	3,378
Percentage Distribution						
Total	100	100	100	100	100	100
Education: 0-11 years	20	23	14	24	21	22
12 years	42	42	42	42	42	41
13 or more years	38	35	44	33	37	38
Welfare Recipients:						
AFDC	16	17	10	18	17	16
Public Assistance, other	7	11	8	10	7	13
Veterans: Total	23	18	21	18	24	18
Vietnam era	8	7	5	7	9	8
Disabled	1	1	1	1	1	1
Handicapped	4	6	4	7	4	5

Source: Data from prime sponsor records. Sample size equals 13 except for education and veteran characteristics where n = 12.

[a]Five prime sponsors reported for only January-March 1979 and three reported for only April-June 1979.

NOTE: Details may not add to 100 percent due to rounding.

of fiscal 1979. In the third and fourth quarters of the year, there was a further decline to 9 percent. The drop appears to have been slightly larger in Title IID than in Title VI; however, the difference is small, only 2 percentage points.

While the preliminary data from the CLMS provide the most reliable information available on the characteristics of newly enrolled PSE participants, this information is available for relatively few characteristics. To gain further insight into the characteristics of participants hired under the reauthorization act, the NAS field observers collected characteristics data on new enrollees in the 28 sample areas. This proved to be a difficult task, and reliable data were obtained in only 13 areas.[5] Nevertheless, the view obtained in these areas is consistent with the information available through the CLMS and the cumulative records on individuals served maintained by the Employment and Training Administration. The sample data for selected characteristics not available from the CLMS are shown in Table 9.

PSE participants hired between January and June 1979 in the 13 sample areas were different in several respects from individuals served in the PSE programs in fiscal 1978. A larger proportion of the new enrollees had less than a high school education, the proportion receiving income transfer payments was up slightly, and the proportion of handicapped individuals was higher. These changes were considerably larger in Title IID than in Title VI. Over the same period, the proportion of veterans among new PSE enrollees declined. This decline, which did not affect Vietnam-era or disabled veterans, was larger in Title VI. These findings are consistent with the changes reported in the characteristics of individuals served nationally in fiscal 1979 (Appendix A, Table A-2).

Twenty-three percent of new PSE enrollees hired between January and June 1979 in the sample areas had less than a high school education, an increase of 3 percentage points over the previous year. Most of this increase occurred in Title IID, where the proportion of persons with less than a high school education rose from 14 to 24 percent. Title VI exhibited an increase of only 1 percentage point. This reflects the fact that prior to the reauthorization act, Title VI served a much larger proportion of persons with less than a high school education (21 percent) than did Title II (14 percent). In addition, the reauthorization act eligiblity requirements represented a much larger departure from the previous criteria in Title II than in Title VI.

The increase in the proportion of enrollees with less than a high school education was entirely offset by a decline in those with 13 or more years of education. Again, this change was confined primarily to Title IID.

Income Transfer Recipients

Despite the special consideration given to AFDC recipients in the reauthorization act, the overall proportion of new PSE enrollees receiving AFDC increased by only 1 percentage point in the 1978 period. This is particularly surprising because women—58 percent of whom are AFDC recipients in the eligible population—made sizeable gains under the reauthorization act. The comparison of all PSE enrollees masks a substantial change in Title IID, where the proportion of AFDC recipients rose from 10 to 18 percent. This increase was partially offset by a 1 percentage point decline in Title VI.

The proportion of public assistance recipients also increased in 1979, from 7 to 11 percent. However, in this case the increase was larger in Title VI (6 percentage points) than in Title IID (2 percentage points).

Handicapped

Handicapped individuals appear to be better represented in the PSE programs in 1979. The proportion of handicapped new enrollees rose from 4 to 6 percent. The increase was somewhat larger in Title IID (3 percentage points) than in Title VI (1 percentage point). However, given the small number of enrollees for which data are available, these differences could be due to sampling variability rather than underlying changes in the characteristics of the population sampled.

Veterans

Total veteran participation in the PSE programs declined in 1979. While 23 percent of the individuals served in fiscal 1978 were veterans, only 17 percent of the new persons enrolled in PSE from January to June 1979 were veterans. However, the specific groups singled out for special consideration in the reauthorization act did not fare as badly. The proportion of Vietnam-era veterans dropped 1 percentage point, a change small enough to fall within the range of sampling variability, and the proportion of disabled veterans remained the same. Veterans appear to have fared better in Title IID than in Title VI. The percentage point decline in total veterans is smaller in Title IID, and the proportion of Vietnam-era veterans increased slightly (2 percentage points). However, this is deceptive. Prior to the reauthorization act, Title VI served a larger

TABLE 10   Number of Newly Enrolled Participants, by Selected
Characteristics, Title II (IID) and Title VI, Fiscal 1978-1979

| Selected Characteristics | Number of New Enrollees Title II (IID) and Title VI | | Percent Change in Number Enrolled |
	Fiscal 1978	Fiscal 1979	
TOTAL NEW ENROLLEES	567,217	395,590	-30.3
Sex: Male	353,265	209,261	-40.8
Female	213,953	186,328	-12.9
Minority Status:			
White (not Hispanic)	345,874	224,222	-35.2
Black (not Hispanic)	166,375	133,080	-20.0
Hispanic	42,453	26,132	-38.4
Other	12,516	12,156	-2.9
Age:			
19 and under	59,222	48,736	-17.7
20-21	72,796	49,480	-32.0
22-44	364,730	256,511	-29.7
45-54	44,327	24,335	-45.1
55 and over	26,141	16,528	-36.8
Economically Disadvantaged	478,876	370,846	-22.6
Receiving unemployment insurance at entry	76,552	36,314	-52.6

Source: Westat, Inc., Continuous Longitudinal Manpower Survey, preliminary data
(unpublished), provided by the Employment and Training Administration, U.S.
Department of Labor.

NOTE: The number of new enrollees for selected characteristics may not add to the
estimated total due to weighting.

proportion of veterans. In 1979, both titles enrolled about the same
proportion of veterans.

Effect of Program Redirection

Although many of the groups traditionally identified as facing disadvantages in the labor market secured a larger share of the available PSE jobs
in fiscal 1979, none of the groups succeeded in gaining enough to offset the
effect of the 30 percent reduction in the size of the PSE programs in fiscal
1979 (Table 10). This situation is likely to intensify in the years ahead.

Some groups, however, clearly did better than others. PSE positions
held by women declined by 13 percent compared to a 41 percent drop for
men. The number of positions filled by blacks declined 20 percent as
compared to 35 percent for whites and 38 percent for Hispanics. The other

minority category, primarily native Americans, fared best of all, experiencing only a 3 percent decline in the number of PSE positions. Enrollment of school age youth turned out to be better than average, the youth having lost only 18 percent of the positions they had held the previous year, while persons age 45 to 54 lost 45 percent of their positions. Unemployment insurance claimants experienced the largest drop of all, a 53 percent decline in PSE positions filled by UI claimants.

Two conclusions can be drawn from these data. First, during a period of reduced program size, it is difficult for any group to benefit from tighter targeting requirements in an absolute sense. Secondly, and more positively, tighter targeting did succeed in distributing the burden of program reductions on those believed to be most able to assume the burden. The reauthorization act provisions did cushion many disadvantaged groups from the full effects of the cut in the size of the PSE programs. This highlights the importance of targeting requirements in a period of declining program size.

DIFFERENCES BETWEEN TITLES IID AND VI

One of the major objectives of the reauthorization act was to establish separate PSE programs serving distinct clienteles. Title IID was to be counterstructural, serving persons in need of employability development, while Title VI was to be countercyclical. Congress built several differences into the two titles that reflect their different objectives. Title IID has:

• more restrictive eligibility requirements in terms of the required length of unemployment before entry, maximum family income, and the period of time over which income is to be annualized;
• a prohibition on wage supplementation unlike Title VI, where supplementation is permitted;
• employability development plans for each participant intended to ensure that the program identifies and meets the needs of the structurally unemployed for training. In addition to these program differences, only Title VI has a cyclical funding trigger that gears funding authorizations to the rate of unemployment. These differences reflect the premise that the clienteles served by the two programs will have differing needs.

An examination of the characteristics of participants hired for Title IID and VI positions in fiscal 1979, however, indicates that the distinction between the two programs is more theoretical than real. Indeed, the

TABLE 11   Selected Characteristics of Newly Enrolled Participants, Title II
(IID) and Title VI, Fiscal 1978 and April-September 1979

Selected Characteristics	Fiscal 1978		April-September 1979	
	Title II	Title VI	Title IID	Title VI
TOTAL ENROLLED	92,978	474,239	104,530	118,858
Percent Distribution				
Total	100	100	100	100
Sex: Male	58	63	49	54
Female	42	37	51	46
Minority Status:				
White (not Hispanic)	68	60	54	54
Black (not Hispanic)	24	30	37	37
Hispanic	6	8	6	5
Other	3	2	3	3
Age:				
19 and under	10	11	14	15
20-21	13	13	14	13
22-44	63	65	61	63
45-54	9	8	6	5
55 and over	6	4	4	4
Economically Disadvantaged	66	89	97	93
Receiving unemployment insurance at entry	14	13	8	9

Source: Westat, Inc., Continuous Longitudinal Manpower Survey, preliminary data
(unpublished), provided by the Employment and Training Administration, U.S.
Department of Labor.

NOTE: Details may not add to 100 percent due to rounding.

reauthorization act has actually reduced the difference between the
clienteles served by the two programs. This is apparent from the CLMS
data (Table 11), which show that:

• although Title IID serves a higher proportion of women than Title
VI, the magnitude of this difference is the same as it was prior to the
reauthorization act;
• the social mixture of new enrollees in Titles IID and VI is identical;
• the age distributions of enrollees in Titles IID and VI were quite
similar in fiscal 1978 and remain so under the reauthorization act;
• the difference in the proportion of economically disadvantaged
participants served by the two programs has shrunk from 23 percentage
points to 4;

TABLE 12   Selected Characteristics of Participants, Title II (IID) and
Title VI, Sample Prime Sponsor Areas, Fiscal 1978 and January-June 1979

Selected Characteristics	Individuals Served Fiscal 1978		New Enrollees January-June 1979[a]	
	Title II	Title VI	Title IID	Title VI
TOTAL ENROLLED	6,480	30,369	4,029	3,378
Percentage Distribution				
Total	100	100	100	100
Education: 0-11 years	14	21	24	22
12 years	42	42	42	41
13 or more years	44	37	33	38
Welfare Recipients:				
AFDC	10	17	18	16
Public Assistance, other	8	7	10	13
Veterans: Total	21	24	18	18
Vietnam era	5	9	7	8
Disabled	1	1	1	1
Handicapped	4	4	7	5

Source: Data from prime sponsor records. Sample size equals 13 except for education
and veteran characteristics where n = 12.

[a]Five prime sponsors reported for only January-March 1979 and three reported for only
April-June 1979.

NOTE: Details may not add to 100 percent due to rounding.

• Titles IID and VI continue to serve roughly the same proportion of
UI claimants, 8 and 9 percent respectively, in fiscal 1979.

The sample data collected by the NRC field observers from prime sponsor
records show a similar pattern (Table 12). The differences between PSE
programs in the proportions of persons who have less than a high school
education, are receiving AFDC, or are veterans have declined from fiscal
1978 to the second and third quarters of fiscal 1979.

In short, PSE participants are a more homogeneous group in fiscal 1979
than they were in 1978. While this implies that there is little justification
for the distinctions that the reauthorization act draws between Titles IID
and VI, it is not an altogether negative finding. The similar clientele that
both PSE programs now serve is the disadvantaged clientele that Congress
has sought to reach through PSE for so long.

FACTORS AFFECTING PARTICIPANT CHARACTERISTICS

The sponsors studied identified the new eligibility requirements and the wage provisions of the reauthorization act as the factors most responsible for the changes in participant characteristics. This section discusses the independent effect of each of these factors on the characteristics of participants.

ELIGIBILITY REQUIREMENTS

The changes in the eligibility requirements mandated by the 1978 amendments sharply reduced the number of persons eligible for PSE positions. In fiscal 1978, almost 19 million persons met the eligibility requirements for Title II and the nonproject portion of Title VI (Population 1, Table 13). Under the least restrictive eligibility provisions established by the reauthorization act, those for Title VI, approximately 6 million persons are eligible (Population 2, Table 13). Thus, Congress has excluded 13 million formerly eligible individuals from participating in the PSE programs. This narrows the choice exercised by local officials in selecting participants and is likely to make it more difficult for prime sponsors to fill positions requiring specialized skills.

At the other end of the spectrum, under the most restrictive provisions of the reauthorization act, Title IID, 4 million persons are eligible (Population 3, Table 13). This is the same number of persons that were eligible under the Title VI project criteria in fiscal 1978, the most restrictive requirements then in effect.

Sex

The new eligibility requirements have clearly increased the proportion of women in the eligible population. In Title IID the shift is quite pronounced, but in Title VI the project and nonproject portions tend to offset each other. The increased proportion of women in the eligible population is consistent with the changes observed in the characteristics of new enrollees, although the increase in the proportion of female enrollees is larger than would be expected by looking only at the changes in the characteristics of the eligible population. This may be due to the fact that enrollment in projects—which were predominantly laboring positions filled by men—has declined as a proportion of total enrollments in fiscal 1979, opening up a larger share of PSE jobs to women. In addition, there has been pressure, both at the federal and local level, to increase the proportion of PSE positions filled by women.

TABLE 13 Characteristics of Populations Eligible for CETA Public Service Employment Programs Before and After the Reauthorization Act (percentage distribution)

	Before Reauthorization			After Reauthorization					
	Population 1			Population 2			Population 3		
Characteristics	Total	Unemployed 30 days	Underemployed	Total	AFDC	Other	Total	AFDC	Other
TOTAL ELIGIBLE (thousands)	18,802	13,835	4,966	5,777	2,327	3,449	4,126	2,327	1,799
Sex: Male	55	59	46	49	27	64	44	27	65
Female	45	41	54	51	73	36	56	73	35
Age: 21 and under	26	27	25	21	16	24	19	16	23
22–44	52	53	48	61	71	54	64	71	55
45 and over	22	20	27	18	13	22	17	13	22
Race/Ethnic Group:									
White and Hispanic	80	82	74	66	59	71	64	59	70
Nonwhite	20	18	26	34	41	29	36	41	30

64

Education: 0–11 years	37	36	37	52	59	47	55	59	50
12 years	42	41	46	35	33	36	33	33	33
13+ years	21	23	17	13	8	17	12	8	17
Economic status:									
AFDC recipient	6	5	8	40	100	0	56	100	0
Economically disadvantaged	43	23	100	78	100	64	100	100	100
Unemployment Insurance Claimant	22	30	2	18	0	29	13	0	30

Source: Unpublished data from the March 1978 Current Population Survey furnished by the Bureau of Labor Statistics; and Table 30, "Characteristics of WIN Registrants" furnished by WIN office of Employment and Training Administration, U.S. Department of Labor. See Appendix B for discussion of methodology.

Definitions: Population 1 – Population eligible for Title II and for Title VI sustainment, before the reauthorization act–population includes persons unemployed 5 weeks or more in 1977 and persons employed 48 weeks or more with family income below the OMB poverty level.

Population 2 – Population eligible under Title VI of the reauthorization act–population includes persons unemployed 10 weeks or more with family income no greater than 100 percent of the BLS low-income standard in 1977 and persons registered with WIN in fiscal 1977.

Population 3 – Population eligible under Title IID of the reauthorization act–population includes persons unemployed 15 weeks or more with family income no greater than 70 percent of the BLS low-income standard in 1977 and persons registered with WIN in fiscal 1977.

NOTE: Eligible populations overlap; persons eligible in one population may also be part of one or both of the other two populations.

Age

The reauthorization act eligibility requirements have reduced the proportion of youth (persons 21 and under) and older workers (persons 45 and older) in the eligible population, despite the intent of Congress that enrollment of these groups in PSE positions be emphasized. The reason for this reduction becomes apparent when the characteristics of non-AFDC eligibles are examined separately. Despite the longer duration of unemployment and lower family income required for eligibility in fiscal 1979, the proportions of youth and older workers in the non-AFDC eligible population are about the same as they were previously. However, the AFDC population has a much lower proportion of youth and older workers. Therefore, because AFDC recipients are an increasingly large proportion of the eligible population, the proportion of youth and older workers in the eligible population is declining. This decline is not consistent with the observed increase in the proportion of youth enrolled in the PSE programs. Other factors, such as the targeting directives in the act or the average wage requirement, may be responsible for the changes in the age distribution of participants.

Race

The reauthorization act has sharply increased the proportion of nonwhites in the population eligible for Titles IID and VI. This reflects not only the larger proportion of AFDC recipients—41 percent of whom are nonwhite—but also the effect of the stricter requirements on income and duration of unemployment. The change is consistent with the objectives of Congress and the changes observed in participant characteristics.

Education

The level of educational attainment dropped sharply among persons in the eligible population under the reauthorization act. This is perhaps the best indication that the new eligibility requirements have succeeded in identifying the structurally unemployed. The shift in the educational attainment of eligibles is congruent with the congressional directive to serve individuals who lack educational credentials. However, a comparison of the magnitude of the changes in the educational attainment of participants with that of persons in the eligible population suggests that this has not been accomplished (see Table 14). Nevertheless, the increase in the proportion of persons with less than a high school education is much larger than in previous years.

TABLE 14   Percentage Point Change in Eligible Population and New
Enrollees for Title IID and Title VI, by Educational Attainment, Fiscal
1978-1979

	Percentage Point Change, Fiscal 1978-1979				
	Title IID		Title VI		
Years of Education	Eligibles	New Enrollees	Eligibles[a] Nonproject	Project	New Enrollees
0-11 years	18	10	15	-3	1
12 years	- 9	0	- 7	2	-1
13 years and over	- 9	-11	- 8	1	1

Source: Tables 9 and 13.

[a]"Nonproject" participants are half of the replacements for regular public service employment positions in 1978. "Project" participants are those enrolled in temporary projects plus half of replacements for regular Title VI public service employment position.

Income

The most striking change in the composition of the eligible population is the sharp increase in the proportion of AFDC recipients. AFDC recipients comprise 40 percent of the population eligible for Title VI and 56 percent of the population eligible for Title IID. Prior to the reauthorization act, only 6 percent of the population eligible for Title II and Title VI nonproject positions were AFDC recipients. It is not clear from the legislative history of the reauthorization act that Congress expected an increase of such magnitude. However, since Congress singled out AFDC recipients as one of two groups to receive special consideration for PSE positions, it is likely that the proportion of AFDC recipients served was expected to increase substantially. This has not yet occurred. Table 9 indicated only a 1 percentage point increase in the proportion of AFDC recipients among new enrollees.

Many factors may tend to constrain the enrollment of AFDC recipients in the PSE programs:

• An AFDC recipient may be reluctant to accept a PSE job given the low wages available, the high marginal tax rate assessed on earnings, and the short-term nature of the work. This reluctance may be compounded by a lack of knowledge or understanding of the many regulations that govern the benefits paid to an AFDC recipient who is employed.

• Lack of coordination and cooperation between the Work Incentive program (WIN) and CETA may inhibit the referral of AFDC recipients to PSE positions. Because WIN does not receive placement credit for a registrant who is referred to CETA and who is subsequently placed by the CETA system, there is a disincentive for WIN to refer anyone to CETA whose prospects for employment appear fairly good. Consequently, WIN referrals are likely to be those AFDC recipients who are least employable and from the standpoint of the prime sponsor least suitable for a PSE job.

• Reluctance on the part of prime sponsors and PSE employers to serve the AFDC population may also inhibit increased enrollment of AFDC recipients. Past studies have documented the importance of a prime sponsor's commitment to serving AFDC recipients if high enrollment levels are to be achieved (U.S. Department of Labor, 1977). Two factors, however, militate against this commitment. First, referral to a PSE job depends on the job qualifications of the applicant. Previous studies have shown that AFDC recipients, even when identified as eligible applicants, are not likely to be referred to PSE positions because they lack the job skills needed. Secondly, some sponsors have indicated their preference to serve individuals who are not receiving transfer benefits, the rationale being that persons receiving cash assistance are not as needy as those without work or income.

Despite the targeting priority given to AFDC recipients, the reauthorization act does little to address the factors that have constrained AFDC participation in the past. It is not surprising therefore that the level of participation by AFDC recipients shows little change.

The proportion of economically disadvantaged, as shown in Table 13, also increased sharply as a result of the new eligibility requirements. Although the magnitude of the change was smaller, the proportion of economically disadvantaged persons enrolled in PSE also increased.

UI Claimants

The stricter requirements on income and duration of unemployment reduced the proportion of UI claimants in the eligible population, particularly in the population eligible for Title IID. This is consistent with the counterstructural emphasis in the IID program and was reflected in the drop in the proportion of IID participants receiving UI.

Summary of Eligibility

The changes in the characteristics of the eligible population are compatible with the objectives of the reauthorization act. The new criteria for income and duration of unemployment increase the likelihood that, with the exceptions of youth and older workers, PSE will serve those persons who face disadvantages in obtaining unsubsidized employment. The changes in the characteristics of persons in the eligible population, for the most part, parallel the changes in participant characteristics examined earlier. However, there are significant differences in the magnitude of the changes. Recipients of AFDC and persons with less than a high school education did not increase their shares of PSE jobs in proportion to their greater representation in the eligible population. On the other hand, youth, a target group whose incidence declined in the eligible population, had a greater proportion of PSE jobs in fiscal 1978 than in the previous year.

WAGE RESTRICTIONS

The average wage requirement is the most controversial of the reauthorization act provisions. The study indicated that lower wages was one of the major factors responsible for the greater proportion of disadvantaged participants in PSE jobs. However, they also suggested that the lower wage made it more difficult to enroll AFDC recipients and veterans who have alternatives that are more attractive than PSE positions.

There are two reasons to believe that the wage restrictions will significantly increase the proportion of disadvantaged individuals participating in PSE. First, lower wages will probably reduce the attractiveness of PSE jobs to persons with alternative sources of income or good prospects for obtaining unsubsidized employment. Thus, persons with marketable job skills will be less likely to accept low-wage PSE positions. Similarly, income transfer recipients will have less of an incentive to accept PSE positions. The second reason is that the lower average wage will make it difficult for prime sponsors to fund many professional and highly skilled positions, especially if the prevailing wage for those positions exceeds the permissible average for the area. As the level of skill required to perform PSE jobs declines, PSE positions will probably become more accessible to the structurally unemployed.

In view of the controversy over the average wage requirement, it is important to know the extent to which the changes in participant characteristics that occurred in fiscal 1979 can be attributed to the average wage requirement. Unfortunately, the available evidence does not present a clear picture.

70

Several techniques were used to test empirically the effects of the average wage requirement on participant characteristics. The characteristics of participants hired under the eligibility requirements before and after the reauthorization act were compared. The correlation between the ratio of the average wage required in fiscal 1979 to the average wage paid in fiscal 1978 was examined in relation to changes in participant characteristics. Furthermore, the timing of the changes in characteristics was scrutinized. None of the techniques produced conclusive results.

The evidence collected by the field research associates is also ambiguous. To determine whether lower PSE wages discouraged some individuals from participating in the PSE programs, CETA administrators were asked about applicants who turned down PSE jobs. Although this study, as well as previous ones, suggests that wage rates affect the willingness of eligible persons to accept PSE jobs, it is not clear whether the new reauthorization act wage provisions have increased the incidence of rejection of PSE jobs. There are several possible explanations: (1) the CETA administrator may not be aware that applicants are turning down jobs; (2) applicants may avoid being chosen for a PSE position without formally rejecting the job; or (3) persons likely to be discouraged by lower wages may never apply for PSE positions.

Prime sponsors identified a number of groups that were more likely than others to turn down PSE jobs. In the order of frequency with which they were mentioned, these groups were unemployment insurance claimants, skilled, job-ready individuals, public assistance recipients, persons with post–high school education, and veterans.

The reasons for applicant rejection of PSE jobs have not changed since the reauthorization act. Both the 1979 field survey and a 1977 survey indicated that four reasons were given when positions were turned down. The reasons are listed in descending order, according to the frequency with which they were cited:

1. PSE wages too low compared with alternate income sources;
2. lack of interest in skill or occupational area;
3. problems relating to transportation or child care; and
4. short-term nature of PSE.

The order was the same in both surveys. Thus, although the data confirm the importance of wage levels in the decision to accept or reject a PSE position, it is not clear whether the lower wages mandated in the amendments have increased the incidence of rejections. Of the sponsors surveyed, 20 percent reported an increase, while 40 percent indicated that the incidence had remained the same. Thirty-two percent did not know whether the incidence of rejections had increased or declined. The latter figure suggests that it may be too early to accurately identify the effects of the wage requirements.

The detailed analysis of PSE occupations in Chapter 4 indicates that, as a result of the wage restrictions (principally the average wage requirement), prime sponsors are increasing the emphasis on occupations requiring fewer skills. Professional, technical, and administrative positions are being de-emphasized, while clerical and laboring positions are receiving more attention. This change is likely to increase the proportion of disadvantaged participants in the PSE programs. Past studies have found that the job qualifications of the applicant were the single most important factor in job referral and hiring decisions (National Research Council, 1980, p. 102; National Research Council, 1978, p. 171). Although PSE employers still seek the most qualified of the available applicants, new PSE jobs require fewer qualifications. Thus, disadvantaged participants are more likely to be referred and hired. This is affirmed by the fact that 68 percent of the CETA administrators in the field study reported that the newly established jobs were more suitable for disadvantaged participants than jobs created previously.

TARGETING GUIDELINES AND SELECTION PRACTICES

Except for tightening the procedures for determining eligibility, the reauthorization has not affected the way in which prime sponsors select PSE participants. The same organizations generally are responsible for recruitment, program assignment, referral, and hiring; they generally do not give preference to the target groups identified in the act. The principal consideration in referral and hiring continues to be the job qualifications of the applicants. This approach tends to exclude those most in need of employment and training services. By restricting the pool of eligible applicants to those most in need, the reauthorization act severely limits the ability of sponsors to select highly qualified participants.

RECRUITMENT

Targeted recruitment is clearly a weak link in the participant selection process. Most prime sponsors rely on a self-selection process—whoever walks in the door is selected if he meets eligibility requirements. As one field research associate pointed out, the neediest populations are the ones least likely to respond to this type of recruitment.

Media advertising and employment service file searches are sometimes used, particularly for a hard-to-fill job. Sixty-eight percent of the sponsors in the field study reported that they attempted to direct their recruitment to specific groups. These efforts, however, appear to be limited. Only veterans and welfare recipients were the targets of special outreach efforts by a significant proportion (36 percent) of the sponsors surveyed.

Two-thirds of the CETA administrators interviewed reported difficulty in recruiting specific target groups. In more than half of these cases the problem was in recruitment of adequate numbers of eligible veterans.

ELIGIBILITY DETERMINATION

The reauthorization act has succeeded in focusing attention on the need to determine eligibility correctly. Nearly half (44 percent) of the sponsors surveyed make additional checks and cross-checks to ensure that persons hired meet the eligibility requirements. This has both benefits and costs. Of those sponsors who reported changes in eligibility determination procedures, 45 percent indicated that the improvements would increase the proportion of disadvantaged participants, particularly low-income, long-term unemployed persons. However, these sponsors also observed that the new procedures require more time and make it more difficult to find eligible applicants (see Chapter 6).

PROGRAM ASSIGNMENT

To determine whether different procedures are used for assigning applicants to the structural and countercyclical PSE programs, NRC research associates asked CETA administrators to identify the factors that influenced the program assignment decisions. Three factors were dominant. Most important was the availability of openings in the program. The applicant's need for employment and training services ranked second, and the job qualifications of the applicant ranked third.

Two conclusions can be inferred. First, the prime sponsor's principal consideration in assigning applicants to PSE programs is the need to keep the job slots filled. This takes precedence over any theoretical differences between Titles IID and VI. In making program assignments, attempts are made to consider applicant needs. To the extent that fewer skills are required for jobs in Title IID, the consideration of the job qualifications of the applicant also tends to promote the assignment of more disadvantaged applicants to Title IID.

REFERRAL AND HIRING

Seventy-six percent of the CETA administrators in the study group reported that the reauthorization act did not affect referral and hiring practices. As in previous surveys, the job qualifications of the applicant were considered to be the most important factor influencing referral and hiring decisions. Only 3 out of 25 sponsors considered the targeting directives of the reauthorization act to be most influential in their referral decisions, and only 2 of the sponsors made their hiring decisions on the basis of the applicant's need for employment assistance.

Past surveys have identified preselection as a factor affecting the hiring decision. In the current survey, an even larger proportion of respondents, 50 percent, indicated that selection of applicants known to the hiring agency is an influential factor in hiring decisions.

In short, the survey findings suggest that recruitment, program assignment, referral, and hiring practices under the reauthorization act have not affected the composition of the population enrolled in PSE programs. However, the new eligibility determination procedures have.

SUMMARY

The tighter eligibility requirements and lower wages mandated by the reauthorization act have directed the PSE programs toward the structurally unemployed. This is evident in the increased participation of women, youth, blacks, and persons from low-income families, as well as in the smaller proportion of unemployment insurance claimants and persons with post–high school education now being hired.

Three groups that Congress expressed special concern for—public assistance recipients, Vietnam-era veterans, and disabled veterans—did not benefit significantly from the reauthorization act. Prime sponsors reported difficulty in finding eligible veterans who were willing to participate. The reasons for the lack of change in the proportion of AFDC recipients participating in PSE are more complex. Inadequate outreach efforts to recruit AFDC recipients, lower-wage PSE jobs, lack of CETA/WIN cooperation, and a referral system that heavily weights the job qualification of the applicant all appear to have played a role in constraining the proportion of AFDC recipients enrolled in PSE jobs.

Under the reauthorization act, Titles IID and VI serve the same clientele—the structurally unemployed. The differences in the eligibility requirements between the two programs are not sufficient to identify eligible populations with significantly different employment and training needs. The principal factor in assignment to Title IID or Title VI is the availability of openings, although sponsors also report evaluating the needs of the applicant. It is still too early to tell, however, whether Title IID and VI will provide substantively different services.

The reauthorization act has had little effect on the process used to select PSE participants. Sponsors continue to rely principally on "walk-ins" for recruitment. When special outreach efforts are made, they are generally directed at veterans or AFDC recipients. However, these efforts are limited, and sponsors report dissatisfaction with the results they produce.

Sponsors have tightened their control over the eligibility determination process. It is anticipated that the greater scrutiny given to participant eligibility will succeed in lowering the incidence of ineligibility, thus directing PSE toward the structurally unemployed. However, the new eligibility determination procedures have increased the time required to process applications. In the event of an expansion of Title VI for countercyclical purposes, these could prove to be a significant source of delay in hiring.

The job qualifications of the applicant remain the single most important factor in the referral and hiring decision. The selection process tends to choose the best qualified applicant available. This suggests the importance of the eligibility requirements and wage restrictions in meeting congressional targeting objectives.

NOTES

1. EJPEA divided the Title VI program into two parts, sustainment and nonsustainment. Sustainment refers to the PSE positions required to maintain the level of enrollment in effect on June 30, 1976. All positions beyond that level were labeled nonsustainment. Under EJPEA, 50 percent of the participants hired to fill vacancies in sustainment positions and all nonsustainment participants were required to meet the tightened eligibility requirements—15 weeks unemployment and family income below 70 percent of the Bureau of Labor Statistics (BLS) lower living standard. In addition, all nonsustainment participants were required to be enrolled in projects. A project consisted of a group of PSE employees performing a discrete task that was separate from regular local government functions and that could be completed in a fixed period of time. The EJPEA eligibility criteria are summarized below:

Eligibility Criteria	Program
(1) Unemployed 30 days	Title II and 50 percent of vacancies in Title VI sustainment
(2) Unemployed 15 weeks and family income below 70 percent of BLS lower living standard income level	50 percent of vacancies in Title VI sustainment and all of Title VI nonsustainment

2. Economically disadvantaged includes persons with family incomes below the Office of Management and Budget level of poverty or 70 percent of the BLS lower living standard, as well as persons who are handicapped or institutionalized.

3. The CLMS is a quarterly national sample of new enrollees in all CETA programs. A full description of the CLMS methodology is contained in Westat, Inc. (1977).

4. Westat estimates that weighted cells of under 7,500 have a standard error in excess of 10 percent.

5. The chief constraints were (1) some prime sponsors had not hired sufficient numbers of new enrollees to obtain a reliable view of participant selection under the reauthorization act requirements, and (2) some prime sponsors were not able to distinguish between intertitle transfers and new enrollees in their reporting systems.

4 Wages, Jobs, and Services

Public Service Employment (PSE) programs were enacted to create temporary jobs for the disadvantaged unemployed. The jobs were to provide useful public services, and the work experience was intended to aid participants in obtaining unsubsidized employment. Despite repeated modifications in the law, Congress and the administration believed that the most disadvantaged in the population were not receiving an adequate share of PSE jobs and were concerned that PSE jobs were substituting for regular government positions. The CETA reauthorization act addressed these problems by restricting enrollment to low-income applicants and the long-term unemployed, and by limiting PSE wages so that PSE jobs would not attract workers who could compete in the regular job market.

These eligibility and wage provisions succeeded in focusing PSE on the seriously disadvantaged and probably reduced substitution. However, they narrowed the range of PSE jobs and limited the services that can be provided. This chapter examines the early effects of the new wage and eligibility requirements on the kinds of jobs and services that prime sponsors provide with PSE funds.

WAGE PROVISIONS IN THE REAUTHORIZATION ACT

The most controversial of the 1978 amendments to CETA were the limitations on the wages to be paid participants. Prior to the reauthorization act, the nationwide average wage for PSE workers was set at $7,800 per year. The maximum wage that could be paid with CETA funds was

$10,000, but there was no limit on the use of local funds to supplement the CETA wage.

These provisions came under sharp attack during the debate on the reauthorization of CETA. Supporters of lower wages argued that new wage limitations would have several advantages:

• The program would be focused more sharply on persons least able to compete in the regular job market;
• Competition between PSE programs and private industry for capable workers would decrease;
• Substitution, the use of PSE for regular government jobs, would diminish;
• Fewer PSE jobs would pay more than the average wages for unsubsidized jobs; and
• The funds appropriated would provide more jobs because the cost per participant would be reduced.

Opponents of lower PSE wages, however, anticipated a number of adverse effects:

• Because wages for PSE jobs must equal local prevailing entry rates for similar work, prime sponsors in high-wage areas would find it difficult to create PSE jobs at the lower PSE wage.
• The creation of low-paying jobs would result in "make-work" rather than the kind of experience that would lead to unsubsidized employment.
• High-wage areas in financial difficulties would be unable to use PSE to provide the kinds of services that communities need but are unable to support with local funds.
• Persons receiving public assistance or unemployment insurance would be less likely to apply for PSE jobs because the net increase in their income would be small or nonexistent.[1] Hence the targeting objective and savings in income transfer payments would not be achieved.

The compromise bill that was finally enacted made the following wage changes:

• The national average wage permitted for PSE was reduced from $7,800 to $7,200 per year for participants entering the program after March 1979 despite the fact that wages for most government and nonprofit organization jobs were rising. For specific areas, the average could be more or less than $7,200 depending on the relation between the national average and the area wage for unsubsidized jobs.[2] The national PSE average wage must be adjusted annually by the percentage change in the average wage for unsubsidized jobs.

- For areas with average or less than average wages, the maximum wage remained at $10,000 per year. However, where wages were above the national average, the permitted maximum ranged up to $12,000.
- Supplementation of CETA wages by PSE employers was significantly limited. No supplementation was permitted for new participants in Title IID programs. (These programs included 43 percent of budgeted PSE positions in 1979.) Supplements for wages under Title VI generally could not exceed 10 percent of the maximum CETA wage for the area; however, in the few areas where average wages for regular jobs were more than 25 percent above the national average, CETA wages could be supplemented by 20 percent. Thus wages after supplementation could be as high as $11,000 in areas where wages do not exceed the average, between $11,000 and $13,200 in most higher-wage areas, and as high as $14,400 per year in a few areas with the highest wages.

EFFECTS OF AVERAGE-WAGE PROVISIONS

The average-wage provisions of the reauthorization act are having a dual effect. They are restricting the program more narrowly to persons who have been least successful in the job market. But they are also changing the nature of PSE jobs and services. Although the lower-wage requirements have resulted in program alterations in most areas, adapting to these provisions was much more difficult for some areas than for others.

Average wages were lowered in four-fifths of the study areas. The reductions average 10 percent and were as much as 20 percent in a few areas. In areas that reduced wages, an average of half of the PSE jobs approved prior to the reauthorization act could not be used for new enrollees because the permissible PSE wages were below the prevailing entry wage for similar unsubsidized jobs. In a few areas about 90 percent of the jobs had to be replaced with lower-wage jobs when on-board enrollees left. At least 2 of the 28 areas exceeded their authorized average wage because of difficulties in developing low-wage jobs.

UNEVEN IMPACT OF AREA WAGE ADJUSTMENT

The 1978 amendments require that the secretary of labor prepare an area wage adjustment index each year. For each area, the national average wage for public service employment must be adjusted by the ratio of the average wage for unsubsidized jobs in the area to the average wage for such jobs in

TABLE 15   Within Area Comparisons of Government and Private Industry
Wages, Selected Occupations, 26 Large Cities, 1977-1978

Occupational Group	Government Wages as a Percent of Private Industry Wages	
	Range	Average
Clerical	78-142	103
Typists, Class B	86-170	111
Skilled Maintenance Group	64-154	100
Helpers, maintenance trades	56-129	97
Janitors, porters, and cleaners	85-158	115

Source: Bureau of Labor Statistics, U.S. Department of Labor, March 1980, Wage
Differences Among Large City Governments and Comparisons with Industry and
Federal Pay, 1977-78, Table 2.

the nation. The adjustment was expected to serve three objectives. In low-
wage areas, reduced PSE wages would help prevent undue competition
with private industry for qualified workers. In high-wage areas, a higher
PSE wage would facilitate use of PSE to provide essential public services in
localities with inadequate tax revenues. Finally, the adjustment was
expected to equalize the difficulties between high- and low-wage areas in
implementing the new wage requirements.

The wage adjustment procedure has not been efficient in serving these
objectives. The adjustment for each area depends primarily on wages in
private industry, which employs 82 percent of all workers, but prior to the
reauthorization about three-fourths of the PSE participants were employed
in government agencies. Geographic variations in private industry wages
do not correlate well with geographic variations in government wages for
low-level jobs.[3] The variation between government and private industry
wages for selected jobs in 26 of the largest cities is illustrated in Table 15.
In New Orleans, the average government wage for clerical workers was 78
percent of the private industry wage for such workers, but in Detroit it was
142 percent. The range is even larger for other occupational groups.

Government wage levels may not correspond with average wages in the
private sector for a number of reasons. The private sector may include a
mix of industries with wages substantially higher or lower than average, or
government wage rates may be appreciably higher or lower than wages for
similar jobs in private industry. These possibilities are illustrated in Gary
and Philadelphia. The highest average PSE wage permitted for the 28
areas in the study was $9,086 for Gary, Indiana. The Gary wage was high
largely because U.S. Steel and other high-wage primary metals plants were

located in the area. However, the lowest wage for manual and clerical workers in the Gary city government was $6,032, or 50 percent less than the PSE average allowed in Gary. The maximum CETA wage that could be paid with federal funds was $12,000, but if hiring agencies chose to supplement the CETA wage, the maximum was $14,400. Under these conditions, a wide variety of PSE jobs similar to city government jobs could be developed.

The adjusted PSE average wage in Philadelphia, on the other hand, was $7,855.[4] Although this was above the national average of $7,200, it was 24 percent less than the lowest wage paid by the city for manual labor jobs ($10,400) and well below the lowest wage for clerical jobs ($9,000). In Philadelphia, wages for jobs in the local government were considerably higher than wages for similar jobs in industry. On the average, municipal wages were 31 percent higher for clerical workers and 14 percent higher for janitors, porters, and cleaners (U.S. Department of Labor, 1980). Under these circumstances, it was not possible to assign PSE workers to city agencies unless new positions could be developed for which there were no comparable positions in the regular job classification structure. However, initial proposals in Philadelphia to restructure jobs and to create trainee positions offering lower pay were opposed by the local union because they were considered a threat to existing wage standards.

Difficulties in Northern and Western Cities

Area wage adjustments have not successfully equalized the impact of the new wage requirements (Figure 5). The adjusted PSE average wage was a greater problem for large cities in the North and West than for those in the South. In the six largest western cities, the PSE average wage was 19 percent below the average entry level wage for such typical lower-skill jobs as typists, class B, refuse collectors, janitors, and laborers. The average entry wage for these jobs in most large northern cities also exceeded the PSE average wage. In the largest southern cities, on the other hand, the PSE average was 3 percent above the entry level wage for these jobs (Table 16). It was difficult for most large northern and western cities to establish PSE jobs similar to jobs existing in city agencies while meeting the requirement to pay prevailing wages. However, in most southern cities, sponsors were able to place PSE enrollees in entry level clerical and manual jobs at wages below the PSE average and therefore could also place other PSE workers in skilled jobs that paid above the average (see Appendix A, Table A-3).

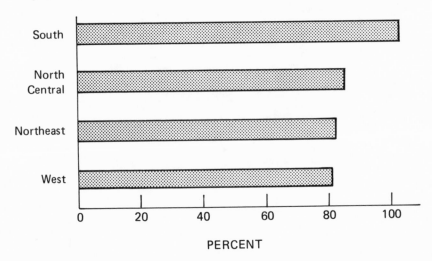

PERCENT

SOURCE: Based on Data from Employment and Training Administration and Bureau of Labor Statistics

FIGURE 5   CETA Public Service Employment Average Wage as a Percent of Entry Wages for Lower-Level City Government Jobs

Wage Competition with Industry

The present procedure is not efficient in preventing wage competition with private industry for workers with saleable job skills. The effect of the 1978 wage restrictions is to limit wages in Title VI programs to a maximum of $11,000 in half the areas and between $11,000 and $13,200 for most of the other areas. For Title IID jobs, the maximum is $10,000 in low-wage areas and between $10,000 and $12,000 in areas with above average wages. PSE positions are not competitive with unsubsidized jobs paying more than these amounts, and few PSE jobs pay the maximum permissible wages because of the average wage requirement. Nonetheless, the presence of high-wage industries in an area will result in a relatively high PSE wage, which may be competitive with the wages for many low-wage jobs in the area. However, if in these areas a portion of the most highly paid jobs were excluded from the wage adjustment, the procedure would probably be more effective in preventing competition with private industry.

TABLE 16   Comparison of CETA Public Service Employment Average Wage and Lowest Wages for Selected Government Jobs in Large Cities, by Region, 1979

Region and City	Permitted Average PSE Wage	Average of Lowest Wages for Selected Government Jobs[a]	PSE Average as a Percent of Low Wage Government Jobs
Northeast			
Boston	$7,805	$ 8,008[b]	97
New York	8,690	10,803	80
Philadelphia	7,855	10,374	76
Pittsburgh	8,129	10,816	75
Average			82
North Central			
Chicago	8,417	11,570	73
Indianapolis	7,920	8,853	89
Detroit	9,662	11,986	81
Kansas City, Mo.	7,553	7,202	105
St. Louis	8,050	7,930	102
Cleveland	8,352	9,295	90
Columbus	7,351	10,660	69
Milwaukee	7,754	10,738	72
Average			85
South			
Washington, D.C.	9,540	9,516	100
Jacksonville	6,667	6,513	102
Atlanta	7,898	7,542	105
New Orleans	7,121	7,020[c]	101
Memphis	6,833	6,562	104
Dallas	7,596	7,332	104
Houston	8,338	7,748	108
San Antonio	6,635	6,622	100
Average			103
West			
Phoenix	6,941	8,528	81
Los Angeles	7,913	9,256	85
San Diego	6,962	9,100	77
San Francisco	8,935	10,261[b]	87
Denver	7,812	9,724	80
Seattle	8,251	10,660[b]	77
Average			81

Source: Permitted average PSE wage from Employment and Training Administration, U.S. Department of Labor. Data on lowest wages for selected jobs computed from Municipal Government Wage Surveys for 1978 and 1979 prepared by the U.S. Bureau of Labor Statistics.

[a]The average of the lowest wage paid for Typist B; Refuse Collector; Janitors, Porters, and Cleaners; and Laborers. See Table A-3 for data on each occupation.
[b]Excludes refuse collectors.
[c]Excludes refuse collectors and janitors, porters, and cleaners.

TABLE 17   Comparison of CETA Public Service Employment and the Long-Term Unemployed, by Occupational Group, 1977 (percentage distribution)

Occupational Group	Public Service Employment[a]	Long-Term Unemployed[b]
ALL OCCUPATIONAL GROUPS	100	100
Total White-Collar	43	33
Professional, technical, and managerial	20	13
Clerical and sales	23	20
Total Blue-Collar	38	43
Craft workers	10	12
Operatives	5	21
Non-farm laborers	23	10
Service workers	18	14
No previous work experience	–	10

Sources: For the unemployed: Bureau of Labor Statistics, U.S. Department of Labor, "Employment and Earnings," January 1978, pp. 146 and 150. For public service employment: Westat, Inc., Continuous Longitudinal Manpower Survey (unpublished data).

[a]Titles II and VI only.
[b]Unemployed 15 weeks or more.

NOTE: Details may not add to 100 percent due to rounding.

PSE WAGES AND JOB CHANGES

Prior to the 1978 amendments, the occupational mix of PSE jobs reflected both the national emphasis on employing the most disadvantaged (one-fourth of the PSE jobs were for laborers) and the local emphasis on providing services that require professional, technical, and managerial skills (one-fifth of the jobs were in these categories). Larger proportions of PSE than of all long-term unemployed were at the extremes of the skill range—either laborers or in the professional, technical, and managerial group (Table 17).

The wage restrictions of the 1978 amendments are expected to shift the PSE occupational mix to a greater concentration of low-skill jobs. Every sponsor in the study whose average wage for public service employment

TABLE 18   Prime Sponsor Perceptions of Effects of Lower Average Wages on CETA Public Service Employment, by Occupation, Sample Prime Sponsor Areas (percent of areas)

Occupational Group	Less Emphasis	No Effect	Increased Emphasis
Professional, technical, and administrative	100	0	0
Paraprofessionals	86	5	10
Clerical workers	10	20	70
Craft workers	85	15	0
Operatives	47	21	32
Laborers	20	5	75
Service workers	10	10	80

Source: Based on reports from 21 areas.

NOTE: Details may not add to 100 percent due to rounding.

was reduced indicated that fewer professional, technical, and administrative jobs would be approved. More than 80 percent of these sponsors also planned reductions in relatively high-skill jobs for paraprofessionals and craft workers. Conversely, sponsors planned to increase the proportion of lower-skill, lower-wage laborer, service, and clerical positions (Table 18).

Data to test sponsors' expectations of the effects of lower wages on PSE occupations were sparse. At the time of the survey, only six areas that provided data on the occupations of participants had enrolled appreciable numbers of PSE workers under the new average wage requirements. These data showed sharp reductions in jobs for professionals and sharp increases in jobs for laborers. However, contrary to sponsors' expectations, the data indicate a somewhat greater incidence of paraprofessional jobs and little change in the proportion of jobs that were in the clerical, craft, and service worker groups.

Plans for achieving the lower average wage involve not only elimination of high-wage jobs, but also restructuring of current positions. Job restructuring (the development of new positions that include only some of the tasks involved in the original positions) was planned in all but one of the areas that reported lower average wages and affected primarily clerical and paraprofessional jobs. High-skill professional, technical, and craft jobs were more likely to be eliminated than redesigned (Table 19).

In some areas, even laboring and service jobs were modified because the prevailing wage for these occupations was above the average CETA wage,

TABLE 19   Local Officials' Opinions of Occupational Groups to be
Dropped and Restructured to Reach Lower CETA Average Wages, Sample
Prime Sponsor Areas (percent of areas)

		Jobs Restructured	
Occupational Group	Jobs Discontinued	Government Agencies	Nonprofit Organizations
Professional, technical, and administrative	87	38	36
Paraprofessionals	70	67	82
Clerical workers	30	71	77
Craft workers	65	29	14
Operatives	13	38	23
Laborers	30	48	23
Service workers	17	33	41

Source: Based on reports from 24 areas.

and a few observers reported that employers went through the motions of changing job titles with little change in job content.

The problem of reaching a lower PSE wage by restructuring relatively low-skill jobs is summarized in a letter to the CETA director in Niagara County, New York, from an official of one of the employee unions (National Association of Counties, 1979, Attachment M):

Most of the attempts at job restructuring can not produce jobs that satisfy the definition in section 675.4 of the CETA regulations, which requires that a restructured job be clearly different from the original job in skills, knowledge, experience *and* ability.

Your proposed "Manual Services Trainee" job description is an attempt to restructure a Laborer job which already requires no special skills, knowledge experience and abilities. . . . in practice, participants working in this title would be doing substantially the same work as laborers earning the higher prevailing wages.

Job restructuring generally was accomplished through creation of subentry level positions such as trainee, aide, assistant, and helper. These trainee positions were established not only for paraprofessional and clerical positions, but also for janitorial and laborer jobs. Because wages in nonprofit agencies were lower than in government agencies, a smaller proportion of jobs in nonprofit organizations had to be restructured.

TABLE 20   Sources of Support for Supervisors of CETA Public Service
Employment Projects, Sample Prime Sponsor Areas (percent of areas)

Support Source	Most Important Source	Sources Used by	
		Government Agencies	Nonprofit Organizations
Funds from employing agency	76	96	93
CETA Program Funds[a]	16	46	68
CETA administrative funds	8	32	39

Source: Based on reports from 27 areas.

[a]CETA participants used as supervisors.

Use of Participants in Supervisory Positions

Because of limited job skills of PSE employees and the requirement that
they receive special employability services, PSE participants require more
supervision than other employees. The cost of such supervision is a
problem for many agencies. When few PSE workers are employed to
expand customary activities, the increased supervisory effort is absorbed
by the agency's regular staff. However, when the PSE activity is a separate
project or involves many enrollees, agencies have usually had to increase
their supervisory staff.

In three-fourths of the study areas, funding for supervisors of PSE
workers has come primarily from employing agencies (Table 20). Agencies
that cannot provide funds to support supervision of PSE participants can
use PSE administrative funds. However, such funds are limited. In fiscal
1979, only 10 percent of a sponsor's PSE allocation could be used for
administration, and many prime sponsors reserved a share of these funds
for their own administrative costs.[5]

Employers can avoid spending their own funds for supervision by using
PSE enrollees for that purpose. In two out of three areas, nonprofit
organizations used PSE participants as supervisors, and in half of the
areas, government agencies followed that practice. However, the new wage
and eligibility restrictions make it difficult to approve supervisory positions
at the wages permitted and to find eligible persons with the required skills.
The wage limitations in the 1978 CETA amendments will force nonprofit
organizations to reduce or eliminate the use of PSE enrollees as
supervisors in half the study areas. Dependence on this source of support
by government agencies will be cut back in 36 percent of the areas.

TABLE 21   Prime Sponsor Perceptions of Effects of Lower Average Wages on CETA Public Service Employment, by Function, Sample Prime Sponsor Areas (percent of areas)

Function	Less Emphasis	No Effect	Increased Emphasis
Law enforcement	79	21	0
Fire protection	58	42	0
Education	47	32	21
Housing	42	53	5
Public works	42	26	32
Health and hospitals	30	50	20
Environment	30	50	20
Creative arts	28	44	28
Social services	26	26	47
Transportation	21	63	16
Recreation and parks	20	20	60

Source: Based on reports from 19 areas.

NOTE: Details may not add to 100 percent due to rounding.

Nonprofit organizations plan to use more of their own funds or will seek other sources to defray supervisory costs. Some sponsors anticipated a reduction in supervision and expected poorer performance and less useful job experience for the enrollees.

EFFECTS OF LOWER AVERAGE WAGES ON PSE SERVICES

The lower average wage is expected to have a major impact on the types of services provided by PSE workers. Public safety services particularly will be affected. About 80 percent of the areas with lowered wages will reduce the use of PSE for law enforcement, and more than half of the areas will cut back PSE fire protection services. Housing activities, primarily weatherization of low-income homes, were expected to be reduced in about 40 percent of the areas.[6] The proportion of PSE funds going to educational services is expected to be smaller in about half of the survey areas but larger in 21 percent of the areas. Recreation and parks and social services will benefit from increased shares of PSE funds (Table 21).

A comparison of the mix of PSE services with all services provided by state and local governments indicates sharp differences before 1978. Nearly 50 percent of state and local government employees worked in

TABLE 22   Comparison of CETA Public Service Employment and All State and Local Government Employment, by Function, 1977 (percentage distribution)

Function	Total State and Local	Total PSE
ALL FUNCTIONS	100	100
Education	49	15
Health and hospitals	11	7
Public works and transportation[a]	12	25
Police and corrections	7	8
Social services	3	12
Parks and recreation	2	13
Fire protection	2	1
Administration and miscellaneous	13	20

Sources: Total state and local employment: U.S. Bureau of the Census, *Public Employment* in 1977, p. 9; PSE data based on unpublished Employment and Training Administration data for Titles II and VI sustainment and on sample of project data summaries for 28 areas for Title VI projects.

[a]Includes highways, local utilities, natural resources, sanitation and transportation.

NOTE: Details may not add to 100 percent due to rounding.

educational activities; only 15 percent of PSE workers were engaged in such services (Table 22). PSE participants were concentrated more heavily than other public sector employees in public works activities and development and maintenance of parks and recreation areas—activities involving high proportions of blue-collar workers. The exception to this pattern was the large share of PSE workers engaged in social service activities, reflecting the sponsorship of PSE activities by nonprofit social service organizations. The reduced emphasis on education and public safety activities and the increased share of PSE for social services and parks and recreation activities will shift the pattern of PSE services further from the general pattern of state and local government activities.

Some areas reported that the wage changes would affect occupations within an activity, but not the distribution of PSE employment among activities. In such instances, the employing agency would replace the higher-level PSE jobs with lower-paying clerical, laborer, and service worker jobs.

INSTITUTIONAL RESPONSES TO LOWER WAGES

Unions

Local labor unions were consulted about the new wage provisions in about 40 percent of the study areas. Union officials were concerned primarily with protecting wage standards. In many areas, consultation led to early resolution of the wage issues and hiring delays were avoided. In one of every six areas where PSE wages were lowered, hiring was temporarily frozen or delayed because of union objections to the proposed PSE wages. In two areas, the union was working with the prime sponsor to develop trainee positions that would justify a lower wage. One area reported that the union agreed to lower entry level wages to save PSE jobs.

Sponsors probably find it more difficult to establish lower-wage jobs in occupations with strong labor unions and formal job hierarchies. This may be one reason the proportion of PSE jobs in law enforcement and fire protection agencies is expected to decrease.

Personnel Systems

In over half of the reporting areas, employing agencies had merit staffing systems that established PSE job descriptions, wage rates, and qualification requirements. However, only one area included PSE workers in a local Civil Service system with all the rights of regular employees.

About three-fourths of the areas reported that no serious issues arose between the prime sponsor and local personnel offices as a result of the lower-wage requirements. In a few areas, however, enrollment delays occurred because some employing agencies resisted job restructuring, and PSE positions had to be transferred to other government agencies or to nonprofit organizations.

SUPPLEMENTATION OF THE CETA WAGE

Prior to the 1978 amendments, there were no restrictions on supplementation of CETA wages. Reports of PSE jobs paying substantially more than the average wage for unsubsidized jobs and concern that CETA funds were being used to finance ongoing operations of local governments led to the restrictions on wage supplementation. The 1978 CETA reauthorization limited supplementation for Title VI enrollees to no more than 10 percent of the maximum CETA wage except in a few high-wage areas where 20 percent was allowed. No supplementation was permitted for new enrollees in Title IID. Persons enrolled prior to October 1, 1978, could

TABLE 23   Extent of Wage Supplementation of CETA Public Service
Employment Positions, Sample Prime Sponsor Areas

Percent of Jobs Supplemented	Percent of Areas with Supplementation
TOTAL	100
0-5	52
6-15	24
16 or more	24

Source: Based on reports from 25 areas.

continue to receive their original wage supplementation as long as they remained in the same PSE position.

In a majority of the study areas, only 5 percent or less of the PSE positions were supported by supplementary funds prior to the reauthorization act (Table 23). However, in a few areas, particularly those in which wages for lower-level government jobs started near or above $10,000, supplementation was extensive. In one large city, over 80 percent of the PSE jobs were affected.

Information on the size of the supplements was available from only six of the study areas where wage supplements were frequently used prior to the reauthorization act. These areas provided data on about 600 supplemented jobs. In these areas, about two-thirds of the supplements were under $2,000, but 8 percent were $5,000 or more. More than half of the supplements exceeded the amount permitted by the reauthorization act (see Table 24).

Prior to the CETA reauthorization, wage supplementation in the six areas was used predominantly to provide funds for PSE jobs that paid more than $10,000. For about 70 percent of the jobs with supplemented wages, the supplement was paid in addition to a CETA-funded salary of $10,000, which was the maximum at the time. More than half of the $10,000 CETA jobs received supplementary employer funding (Table 25).

The effect of the supplementation limits on PSE jobs and services was similar to the impact of lower average wages but weaker. Only 2 of the 28 areas in the study reported that the supplementation limits had a greater influence on jobs and services than the other wage changes in the 1978 amendments. Nearly all study areas were affected by the restraints on supplementation, but in most instances, only a small share of PSE jobs could not be refilled when vacancies occurred. In 4 out of 5 areas, some professional or technical positions were scheduled to be dropped because

TABLE 24   Supplemented CETA Public Service Employment Positions, by Amount of Supplementation, Sample Prime Sponsor Areas

Amount of Supplementation	Percent of Supplemented Jobs[a]
TOTAL	100
$1-999	37
$1,000-1,999	31
$2,000-4,999	23
$5,000 or more	8
Percent of jobs supplemented in excess of amount permitted under the reauthorization act	53

[a]Average percent for 6 areas. Based on occupational summaries prepared in the spring or summer of 1979; refers to persons enrolled prior to October 1978 who were still employed after March 1979.

TABLE 25   Supplemented CETA Public Service Employment Positions, by Wage Class, Sample Prime Sponsor Areas

CETA Wage	Percent of all Jobs With Supplementation[a]	Percent of all Enrollees in the Wage Class with Supplementation[a]
Under $9,000	7	2
$9,000-9,999	21	11
$10,000 or more[b]	72	56

[a]Average for 6 prime sponsors. Based on occupational summaries prepared in the spring and summer of 1979; refers to persons enrolled prior to October 1978 who were still employed after March 1979.
[b]A few jobs with a CETA wage greater than $10,000 were reported for persons enrolled prior to October 1978. These can occur due to cost of living or time in grade raises after the reauthorization.

the prevailing wages for similar jobs were higher than the permitted PSE wage including supplementation. In more than half of the areas, paraprofessional and craft positions would not be continued. Most of the impact would be felt in government agencies. Few PSE jobs with nonprofit organizations provided wage supplementation, and more than half of the study areas reported that the number of discontinued positions with nonprofit agencies would be negligible.

Law enforcement was again the hardest hit activity. More than half of the areas reported that the share of PSE jobs located in law enforcement agencies would be reduced as a result of the limits on wage supplementation. Fire protection jobs were affected in a third of the areas. Prior to the reauthorization act, supplemented PSE salaries for policemen and firefighters ranged from $11,500 to $17,500.

In recent years, there has been intense interest in better law enforcement, and police chiefs have reported that a 27 percent increase in staff would be needed to satisfy community expectations (National Planning Association, 1977, p. 79). PSE jobs in law enforcement contributed to higher levels of services, but the high wages paid to PSE police officers in some areas suggest that CETA funds were sometimes used to pay salaries for police department jobs that would have been funded by local revenues had CETA funds not been available.

INCREASED MAXIMUM WAGE

To allow some flexibility in using PSE positions for essential activities in high-wage areas, the 1978 amendments permitted the maximum wage that could be paid from CETA funds to range up to $12,000 for areas with above-average wages and retained the $10,000 maximum wage for all other areas.

The higher maximum wage had little effect on PSE jobs and services because in most areas the average wage requirement determined the types of jobs and services that could be provided. To stay within the average wage limits, sponsors had to offset jobs paying above-average wages with jobs paying below the average. The increased maximum was the most important wage change in only one of the areas in the study. In some areas, the higher CETA maximum was used to provide scheduled pay increases or cost-of-living increases for PSE participants. In the majority of areas with increased maximum wages, only PSE participants employed by government agencies benefited.

The act provides for annual adjustments in the average wage but not in the maximum wage. Although the average wage exercises the dominant influence on the kinds of jobs that can be established, a fixed maximum wage in a period of wage increases will reduce the range of jobs that can be approved for PSE.

CHANGES IN PARTICIPANT SKILLS AND EFFECTS ON JOBS AND SERVICES

Applicants for PSE jobs in the summer of 1979 were considered less qualified than those of a year earlier in three out of four reporting areas. The decrease in the level of qualifications was attributed to the more restrictive eligibility criteria and to the unwillingness of better qualified eligibles to take PSE jobs at the wages offered. The reactions of employers to the poorer qualifications of PSE participants are reflected in the following comments: "The wage restrictions ensure targeting to the hardcore unemployed," and "PSE is now restricted largely to the unemployables." Some hiring agencies are asking, "Is it worth it?"

In about two-thirds of the areas, the decrease in skills was expected to affect the types of jobs that could be included in PSE programs. Sponsors planned to replace professional, technical, and craft jobs with entry level clerical, custodial, and laboring jobs and expected that it would be more difficult to find applicants for PSE jobs who were able to supervise other PSE enrollees. Education, health, and home weatherization were cited as services that would be particularly affected.

NONPROFIT ORGANIZATION SPONSORSHIP OF PUBLIC SERVICE EMPLOYMENT

Congress has consistently favored extensive use of nonprofit organizations in the CETA program. The Conference Report on the 1976 amendments stated, "The conferees expect prime sponsors to provide a substantial portion of project funds to nonprofit agencies . . . " (U.S. Congress, 1976c, p. 17). The conferees believed that use of nonprofit organizations for public service employment would reduce substitution and would broaden the types of jobs and services provided by PSE programs. These expectations were met. The use of nonprofit organizations increased substantially during the 1977-1988 PSE expansion. Two recent studies indicate that substitution is less of a problem in nonprofit organizations than in government agencies (National Research Council, 1980, p. 130; National Commission for Employment Policy, 1979, pp. 27 and 39).

Although the 1978 amendments did not specifically require an expanded role for nonprofit organizations, the more restrictive wage provisions were expected to necessitate greater use of these organizations. Nonprofit organizations could develop low-wage jobs more easily than government agencies that were more likely to have formal personnel systems and agreements with labor organizations.

In three-fourths of the reporting areas, nonprofit organizations em-

94

ployed a larger proportion of PSE participants than they had prior to the reauthorization act. In May 1979, 34 percent of all PSE jobs were in nonprofit organizations as contrasted with 24 percent in September 1977. About two-thirds of the study areas expected the trend to continue, particularly after September 1979, when the PSE employees hired prior to the reauthorization act would be dropped from the program.

Increased use of nonprofit organizations was attributed to low PSE wages in 64 percent of the areas and to more restrictive eligibility criteria in 45 percent of the areas. In a majority of areas the difficulty of developing lower-wage PSE jobs in government agencies resulted in the allocation of more jobs to nonprofit organizations. In a few areas, where wages in nonprofit organizations were as high as those in government, there was little or no shift to nonprofit organizations. Some respondents reported that nonprofit organizations were more willing than government agencies to employ the less skilled workers that were available after the tighter eligibility requirements became effective.

"Proposition 13" was a factor in the greater use of nonprofit organizations in California. Two of the four California areas in the study reported that supervisors could not be made available for PSE because of the limits on employment in local governments. In San Joaquin County, a successful youth employment project could be expanded only by shifting responsibility to a nonprofit organization.

PSE JOBS AND SERVICES IN NONPROFIT ORGANIZATIONS

The National Research Council study of the expansion of PSE after the Economic Stimulus Act of 1977 found that Title VI project positions in government agencies differed sharply from Title VI positions in nonprofit organizations (National Research Council, 1980, pp. 146-150). Government agencies were heavily engaged in public works and the development and maintenance of park and recreation facilities. Nonprofit organizations directed their PSE programs primarily to social services and housing activities (largely "weatherization"). They also devoted more of their projects to creative arts and to health and hospitals than did government agencies (Table 26).

The occupations used in government agency and nonprofit organization projects reflected the differences in their PSE activities. Government agency projects employed a high proportion of blue-collar workers, primarily laborers in public works and parks activities. Nonprofit organizations, heavily involved in social service, creative arts, health, and teaching activities, have required relatively high proportions of profession-

TABLE 26   Title VI Project Employment, by Function, by Government
Agency and Nonprofit Organization, 1977 (percentage distribution)

Function	Government Agency	Nonprofit Organizations
ALL AREAS	100	100
Public works	33	3
Parks and recreation	21	9
Education	19	13
Social services	8	40
Law enforcement	5	2
Housing	4	15
Health and hospitals	3	8
Creative arts	a	7
Other	5	3

SOURCE: Expanded to U.S. total based on a sample of project data summaries for 28
study areas.

[a]Less than 0.5 percent.

NOTE: Details may not add to totals due to rounding.

al and paraprofessional workers. Only 5 percent of the total PSE
participants employed by nonprofit organizations were laborers (Table 27).

Despite their higher-skill occupational structure, nonprofit organizations have greater flexibility than government agencies in adjusting to
lower PSE wages. Greater use of nonprofit organizations is likely to result
in more emphasis on social services for the poor and the elderly and
expansion of home weatherization programs.

Public officials in a few areas believed that transition to unsubsidized
jobs was less likely to result from PSE jobs in nonprofit organizations than
from PSE jobs in government because nonprofit organizations had fewer
permanent staff openings and did not provide the kinds of job experience
that were transferable to private industry. The available information did
not permit a direct comparison of the placement rate of nonprofit
organizations with that of government agencies. However, the data that
are available do not support the view that PSE workers in nonprofit
agencies are less likely to obtain unsubsidized employment. The placement
rate is influenced by many factors, including the unemployment rate, the
skill of job placement personnel, and the characteristics of enrollees. Half
of the participants in the PSE projects sponsored by nonprofit organiza-

TABLE 27   Title VI Project Employment, by Occupational Group, by Government Agency and Nonprofit Organization, 1977 (percentage distribution)

Occupational Group	Government Agency	Nonprofit Organizations
ALL OCCUPATIONAL GROUPS	100	100
Total White-Collar	35	62
Professional, technical, and managerial	10	25
Paraprofessionals	12	26
Clerical workers	13	11
Total Blue-Collar	58	27
Craft workers	17	19
Operatives	3	4
Laborers	39	5
Service workers	8	11

SOURCE: Expanded to U.S. total based on a sample of project data summaries for 28 study areas.

NOTE: Details may not add to totals due to rounding.

tions were professional, technical, administrative, and paraprofessional workers. These workers are more likely than low-skill workers to obtain regular employment. When the percentage of PSE jobs sponsored by nonprofit organizations and the additional variables were introduced into a multiple regression model, the effect of greater dependence on nonprofit organizations did not significantly affect the placement rate.

THE USEFULNESS OF PSE SERVICES

Advocates of public service employment have insisted that the program provide useful public services as well as temporary employment. Local governments, especially those in fiscal distress, seek to use PSE to provide services that cannot be financed from local tax revenues. Congressional concern that PSE provide useful services was emphasized in the debate that preceded the 1976 amendments of CETA. More recently, the House Appropriations Committee report on the DOL-HEW budget requested the secretary of labor "to explore means of increasing the assignment of CETA public service job-holders to projects that produce lasting benefits to the society at large by increasing our nation's capital assets. This could include work on roads, bridges, parks and trails, among others." (U.S. Congress, 1979b).

Because there is no market price for many of the services provided by PSE, it is difficult to establish an objective measure of their value. In a previous NRC study, perceptions of usefulness were obtained from local officials who were familiar with specific Title VI projects in their community. Ninety-five percent of the respondents identified the projects as very useful. (National Research Council, 1980, pp. 138-139).

The usefulness of the PSE services was expected to be adversely affected by the 1978 CETA amendments in almost all of the study areas. In one-seventh of the study areas, one or more local governments within a prime sponsor area was considering dropping out of the program because of reduced benefits and increased operating difficulties. However, local officials in a majority of the areas emphasized that most PSE activities continued to provide important benefits to their communities. Usefulness had diminished, but had not been eliminated. Some officials expressed concern that the new PSE jobs did not provide the kind of experience that would help participants obtain unsubsidized employment. In a few areas, additional staff experience or a smaller size program resulted in improvements in the effectiveness of the activities despite the wage and eligibility restrictions in the 1978 amendments.

The wage restrictions were far more important than the skills of the participants in limiting the usefulness of PSE activities. About 70 percent of the sponsors in the study group believed that PSE usefulness was limited primarily because the allowable CETA wage precluded the kinds of jobs necessary to provide high-priority services. Twenty-one percent said the inadequate skills of the participants were the most important factor (Table 28).

LOWER AVERAGE WAGES AND USEFULNESS OF ACTIVITIES

All but one of the areas with lowered PSE wages in 1979 anticipated a decline in the utility of PSE services. Many positions in high-priority activities such as police and fire protection, home winterization, and education are scheduled to be replaced by entry level and subentry level positions that are considered less useful to the community. Furthermore, the number of low-skill jobs that can be used effectively in an agency is limited.

In about half the areas with lower wage rates, the usefulness of PSE activities was also adversely affected because eligible persons with job skills were rejecting the low-wage jobs. The PSE wage attracted only persons with poor job skills. However, in some areas the shift to less essential, low-

TABLE 28 Local Officials' Perceptions of Factors Limiting the Usefulness of CETA Public Service Employment Activities, Sample Prime Sponsor Areas (percent of areas)

Factors	Most Important	Second Most Important
ALL REPORTS	100	100
Wage limits	71	21
Participants' job skills	21	46
Termination requirements for Title VI projects	0	11
Limits on administrative expenditures	0	14
None are important	7	7

Source: Based on reports from 28 areas.

NOTE: Details may not add to 100 percent due to rounding.

skill jobs occurred despite the availability of eligible persons who were qualified for positions in high-priority activities.

Several respondents indicated that the lower average wage had been in effect for too short a time to determine the long-term impact on usefulness. The major impact would be felt only after September 1979, when participants enrolled prior to the reauthorization act complete their tenure and are replaced by participants subject to the lower wage provisions.

JOB PERFORMANCE OF PSE PARTICIPANTS

Perceptions of the job performance of PSE workers were less favorable in 1979 than in 1977. Two-thirds of the local officials contacted, including CETA administrators and officials of employing agencies, reported that the job performance of PSE enrollees was about the same as that of regular employees doing similar work. However, the remaining third considered PSE workers "below average." Only 16 percent of the respondents in the 1977 survey rated PSE workers as below average, and an almost equal number ranked them as "above average" (Table 29).

SUBSTITUTION

The fear that "substitution"—the use of PSE funds for jobs that otherwise would be supported by local resources—would undermine the creation of new jobs was reflected in the CETA legislation and in the predecessor

TABLE 29 Rating of Job Performance of CETA Public Service Employment
Workers, 1977 and 1979 (percent of respondents)

Rating	1977 Survey[a]	1979 Survey[b]
Below average	16	32
About average	71	68
Above average	13	0

[a]117 respondents from 27 areas.
[b]78 respondents from 26 areas.

program, the Emergency Employment Act of 1971. These statutes have
included "maintenance of effort" provisions—requirements that employing agencies shall not reduce their regular work force by hiring PSE
workers. The 1976 amendment to CETA attacked the substitution
problem by requiring that expansion of Title VI PSE jobs be limited to
special short-duration projects that would emphasize new or separately
identifiable tasks rather than the expansion of ongoing activities. Additionally, a "substantial portion" of project funds was to be directed to
nonprofit organizations and eligibility for project jobs was tightened.

The 1978 amendments took a different tack. Rather than trying to define
permissible activities, they tightened wage and eligibility criteria to
produce changes in the kinds of people participating in PSE programs and
the kinds of services provided by the programs; in turn these changes were
expected to reduce the incentives for substitution. These restrictions have
had the following results:

- There is less use of PSE in the primary government functions of
public safety and education where the likelihood of substitution is greatest.
- The shift to lower-skill jobs moves PSE further from the pattern of
regular governmental activities.
- The enrollment of the more severely disadvantaged persons reduces
the likelihood that PSE workers will be used in lieu of regular government
workers.
- Low wages are inducing a shift of PSE from government agencies to
nonprofit organizations that are less likely to use PSE participants for their
regular positions.[7]

This study made no attempt to measure changes in the incidence of
substitution. However, it is inferred that the lower wages and tighter

eligibility requirements have produced program modifications that probably have reduced the extent of substitution.

SUMMARY

Both the advocates and the opponents of lower PSE wages correctly anticipated its effects. Lower wages are serving the purposes for which they were designed: they, along with the new eligibility criteria, are focusing the program on persons who have the most difficulty in obtaining unsubsidized jobs; PSE less often competes with private industry for qualified workers; and the opportunities for substitution have been reduced.

Offsetting these benefits, however, the public services provided by PSE are less useful than those provided prior to the 1978 amendments. Preferred activities are being replaced with lower-priority services. In areas where wages for many low-level government jobs are above the PSE average, it has become difficult or impossible to use new PSE enrollees for needed services that cannot be supported within regular budgets. Some officials believe that the new PSE jobs do not provide the type of experience that will help participants obtain regular jobs.

Despite the difficulties in creating PSE positions within the constraints of the wage restrictions, PSE enrollment increased from 546,000 at the end of March to an estimated 570,000 at the end of June; but this growth was 9 percent short of the 625,000 goal.[8]

The lower average wages required by the CETA reauthorization are having a major impact on the types of jobs and services provided by PSE and on the usefulness of PSE activities.

• Twenty-three of twenty-eight reporting areas were required to reduce the average wage for new PSE participants.

• In areas where average wages must be lowered, use of PSE for high-skill professional, technical, paraprofessional, and craft jobs will be reduced.

• Almost all areas that were required to reduce their average wages planned to restructure PSE jobs. Restructuring will generally involve intermediate-skill paraprofessional and clerical occupations, but even low-skill service worker and laborer jobs will be redesigned in some areas because the prevailing entry wage for these positions exceeds the PSE wage that can be approved. Professional and craft jobs are more likely to be discontinued than restructured.

• The PSE activities that will most frequently be cut back are those involving the primary governmental services of law enforcement, fire protection, and education. An increased portion of PSE will support the development and maintenance of parks and recreation facilities and will require a high proportion of workers in unskilled laboring jobs. More PSE positions will be devoted to providing social services, largely through nonprofit organizations.

• The share of the PSE program contracted to nonprofit organizations has increased from 24 percent in 1977 to 34 percent in 1979 primarily because nonprofit organizations can meet the lower PSE wage more easily than government agencies.

• Local officials in three-fourths of the study areas believe that lower average wages are having an adverse effect on the usefulness of PSE services; higher-priority activities will be dropped and lower-priority activities will be substituted.

The effect of the PSE average wage varies among geographic areas. the PSE average wage for the largest western cities was 19 percent below the entry wages for low-level jobs in government; for the largest southern cities, the PSE average was 3 percent higher than the entry wages for low-level government jobs.

The lower PSE wages and the tighter eligibility requirements have affected the qualifications of PSE participants and the types of skills needed for PSE employment and may have reduced substitution.

• New PSE participants possessed fewer job qualifications than those enrolled prior to 1979 in three-fourths of the study areas. Lower wages and more restrictive eligibility were responsible in an equal number of areas.

• Fewer skills are required to perform PSE jobs because the lower wage prevents the funding of many higher-level jobs.

• Two-thirds of the CETA administrators and officials of agencies that employ PSE workers assess the job performance of PSE workers as about the same as other employees doing similar work. The remaining third reported that PSE workers were below average. Perception of worker performance was less favorable in 1979 than in 1977.

• Lower PSE wages probably reduce substitution for several reasons: jobs in high-priority public services are reduced; fewer new enrollees have the qualifications required for regular government jobs; and an increased proportion of PSE jobs are sponsored by nonprofit organizations, which are less likely than government agencies to use PSE participants to replace regular workers.

NOTES

1. A survey of eight prime sponsor areas in 1977 found that the financial incentives for PSE jobs ranged from $1.00 to $1.46 for welfare recipients and from a loss of $0.46 to a gain of $1.36 per hour for former unemployment insurance beneficiaries. See U.S. General Accounting Office (1978), p.4.

2. Among the contiguous 48 states, average PSE wages ranged from $6,635 (10 percent above the federal minimum wage) for parts or all of about one-third of the prime sponsor areas, to more than $10,000 for two areas in Michigan.

3. For fiscal 1979, the adjustment factor was based on private industry wages only. However, because government employees comprise only 18 percent of total wage and salary workers in the United States, the inclusion of their wages in 1980 and later years will not have a significant impact, except in a few areas where there are large concentrations of government workers.

4. In 1978, average hourly earnings in manufacturing were $6.53 in Philadelphia and $9.43 in the Gary–Hammond–East Chicago area. (U.S. Department of Labor, 1979b).

5. PSE funds for administration could be pooled with administrative funds for other CETA programs in 1979 so that more or less than 10 percent may have been available for PSE.

6. Employment and Training Administration Field Memorandum 463-79 of September 26, 1979, provides instructions for increased cooperation of CETA programs with those of the Department of Energy and the Community Services Administration to expand weatherization efforts.

7. The Brookings Institution study of PSE found that displacement of regular workers was 22 percent in government agencies but only 4 percent in nonprofit organizations. See National Commission for Employment Policy (1979), pp. 27 and 39.

8. Reported enrollment increased sharply between May and June 1979, from 561,000 to 592,000, but the data are believed to include an estimated 22,000 summer program enrollees.

5 Transition and Employability Development Services

THE REAUTHORIZATION ACT

The transition of participants from federally subsidized jobs to unsubsidized employment has, with some exceptions, been a cardinal feature of public service employment programs. Indeed, placements have become the measure by which the short-term effectiveness of employment and training programs is judged. The Emergency Employment Act of 1971 contained rigorous transition requirements that were carried over to Title II of the original CETA legislation. However, with the addition of Title VI, enacted during the 1974-1975 recession, the emphasis on placements became secondary to the speedy implementation of the new countercyclical job creation program. The Emergency Jobs Programs Extension Act of 1976 further weakened the transition objectives of CETA by explicitly barring the secretary of labor from setting any specific transition goals for prime sponsors.

The reauthorization act of 1978 revives the emphasis on transition. Although it does not prescribe quotas or goals, it contains several provisions that are directed toward increasing the proportion of Public Service Employment (PSE) participants who move into unsubsidized jobs when they leave the program. The act (Sect. 232(a)) requires that Title IID PSE jobs " . . . be combined with training and supportive services . . . and . . . be designed to enable participants to move into unsubsidized employment." Under the act, the percentage of Title IID funds that must be devoted to training ranges from 10 percent in fiscal

103

1979 to 22 percent in 1982. Similar restrictions are imposed on Title VI spending; at least 10 percent of 1979 funds and 5 percent of all future funds must be used for training and services to develop the employability of participants. To ensure that congressional intent would be carried out, the act limits the tenure of PSE participants to 18 months, authorizes the secretary of labor to establish performance standards, and requires prime sponsors to set performance and placement goals.

This chapter explores the probable impact of the reauthorization act changes on transition, describes the plans, strategies, and management practices developed by sponsors to accomplish their transition objectives, and analyzes the current trends in job entry rates.

Unfortunately, empirical data that permit a comparison of transition rates before and after the reauthorization act provisions are not yet available. The termination data obtained through September 1979 do not include information on sufficient numbers of people who were subject to the new reauthorization requirements to provide an accurate picture of its full effects.

ANTICIPATED EFFECTS OF THE REAUTHORIZATION ACT

As a result of the new provisions in the 1978 amendments, the proportion of PSE enrollees who obtain unsubsidized jobs is expected to increase. The requirement that prime sponsors set placement goals may encourage sponsors to step up transition efforts, and the prescribed employability development plans and training should help PSE workers obtain unsubsidized employment. The most important provision, however, will probably be the 18-month limit on participation in PSE programs.

According to the prime sponsors in our study, the amount of effort participants will make to find unsubsidized employment is influenced primarily by their perceptions of the security of PSE jobs. Participants who recognize the temporary nature of PSE jobs are more likely to begin a job search. Despite the 18-month limit, however, several prime sponsors reported that it is difficult to convince participants that PSE jobs are short-term.

Limited PSE tenure was also the most important factor motivating employers to move PSE workers into regular jobs. Transition is constrained, however, by the number of vacancies in the employer organization and the concern of employers that PSE positions that have been vacated will not be refilled. Some employers hesitate to move PSE workers into unsubsidized positions because the new wage restrictions make it difficult to refill positions. One research associate described the constraints in this way:

TABLE 30   Local Officials' Perceptions of the Effects of CETA Provisions on Transition of Public Service Employment Participants to Unsubsidized Jobs, Sample Prime Sponsor Areas (percent of areas)

Provision	Increase Transition	Decrease Transition	No Effect on Transition	Don't Know
Limits on duration of participation	78	11	11	0
Eligibility requirements	0	68	32	0
Wage limitations	36	32	25	7
Use of PSE for essential services	54	18	28	0
Enrollment objectives	7	28	61	4

Source: Based on reports from 28 areas.

. . . the moratorium placed by the prime sponsor on the PSE program makes employing agencies reluctant to transition workers or have them find their own jobs because there will not be another PSE worker available to fill that job. And chances are that the job left unfilled pays more than the [now lower] average wage permits, so that the position will never be PSE staffed again.

The effect of lowered average wages on refilling vacant PSE positions may diminish as PSE jobs are restructured to meet the new requirements. However, if the restructured positions do not provide training and job experience that is relevant to the labor market, transition opportunities will be adversely affected.

There is, however, a fundamental trade-off between the commitment to serve a greater proportion of disadvantaged persons in PSE and the pursuit of transition; frequently, the most disadvantaged persons are the least employable.

Sponsors agree that limitations on the duration of participation in PSE will serve to increase transition to unsubsidized employment and that the tighter eligibility requirements are likely to decrease transition (Table 30). There is no consensus, however, about the effects of the wage provisions. Some sponsors believe that the wage limitations will increase participation by those most difficult to place and thus reduce transition possibilities; others expect the lower PSE wages to serve as an incentive for participants to seek more attractive unsubsidized jobs. Both factors are likely to be operating.

At least three other factors are believed to affect transition rates: (1) the use of CETA workers to provide essential services, (2) higher enrollment objectives, and (3) the use of projects under Title VI. Under the original CETA legislation, the prospect of using PSE workers to support essential local services was an incentive to sponsors for participating in the program. Although reliance on PSE workers to provide such essential services may induce substitution, especially in areas facing fiscal stringencies, the relevancy of the positions and the skills obtained in these jobs may increase the possibilities for transition.

Periodically, PSE programs have been sharply increased in response to rising unemployment. It has been suggested that the pressures on prime sponsors to reach higher enrollment levels have made some of them reluctant to terminate participants and jeopardize their enrollment and expenditure targets. While most of the sponsors in our study do not believe that enrollment objectives adversely affect transition, more than one in four does.

Under Title VI, at least 50 percent of the funds must be used for projects planned to last for not more than 18 months. The duration of projects was extended from 12 to 18 months under the reauthorization act to conform to the limits on participant tenure. Since projects are intended to be temporary undertakings and not part of the normal activities of employers, opportunities for participants to move into unsubsidized jobs with their PSE employers may be limited.

PLACEMENT EXPERIENCE

Job entry rates have become the customary measure of the short-run effects of employment and training programs. They have the advantage of being relatively objective and easy to compute, but they are marred by serious conceptual problems and data limitations.

All individuals who leave PSE programs during the year are classified as "terminations" and put into one of four categories:

• *Entered Employment.* Persons placed in unsubsidized jobs by prime sponsors, persons who found such employment on their own, or persons who entered the armed forces.[1]
• *Other Positive Termination.* Persons who enrolled in school or a non-CETA employment or training program.
• *Transfer to Other Title.* Persons who were transferred to programs operated under other CETA titles.
• *Nonpositive Termination.* Persons who did not obtain other employment, were not transferred to another CETA program, and did not enroll in school, the armed forces, or other training.

Persons classified as entering employment are subcategorized based on the extent of placement services they received. *Direct placements* represent persons who received only minimal services, such as counseling, and were placed without having entered PSE employment. *Indirect placements* are persons who obtained unsubsidized employment as a result of prime sponsor or subgrantee efforts. *Self-placements* (other indirect placements) represent persons who find employment on their own or through means other than those provided by the sponsor or its agent. Even though self-placements are not attributable to prime sponsor placement activities, it should be noted that they may be the culmination of good counseling and training and an appropriate PSE assignment.

The job entry rate, as used in this report, represents the ratio of the number of participants who entered employment to the total number of program terminations excluding persons transferred to other titles. Gross job entry rates may not fully reflect placement performance since distinctions are not made between differences in the kinds of persons placed, the nature and duration of their jobs, or the state of the labor market.

DATA LIMITATIONS

In addition to the conceptual problems, there are difficulties with the job entry data that stem from the manner in which changes in the employment status of terminees are handled. Some sponsors put terminated employees on "hold" status until they find an unsubsidized job. A recent GAO report noted that " . . . such inaccuracies can significantly distort the reliability of the reports" (U.S. General Accounting Office, 1979, p. 40). It cited a report of the Dallas prime sponsor, indicating that terminations were understated by 140, and job entry rates were, therefore, artificially high.

Sponsors may change the reported employment status of terminees within 90 days of termination if the individual's situation changes. Some sponsors routinely follow up and record job entries that are made during this period, while others do not. National Continuous Longitudinal Manpower Survey (CLMS) data indicate that employment status changes during that period could be substantial (Westat, Inc., 1979, p. 5-2):

About half of those who were unemployed at termination and about three-fifths of those who were not in the labor force had changed their status by the three month post-termination time point. . . . 30 percent of the terminees who were employed at termination were either unemployed or out of the labor force three months later.

Thus, sponsors with identical job entry experiences could report job entry rates that are over 50 percentage points apart if they have different follow-up policies.

TABLE 31 Job Entry Rates, Title IID and Title VI, by Type of Prime Sponsor, Sample Prime Sponsor Areas, Fiscal 1978-1979

Type of Prime Sponsor	Title IID			Title VI			Total Titles IID and VI		
	Fiscal 1978[a]	January-June 1978[a]	January-June 1979	Fiscal 1978	January-June 1978	January-June 1979	Fiscal 1978	January-June 1978	January-June 1979
National Job Entry Rates[b]	45	44	47	33	33	36	35	35	39
Study Sponsor Job Entry Rates[c]									
City	43	42	45	34	34	36	35	35	39
County	40	43	27	31	34	26	32	35	27
Consortium	49	48	53	35	35	44	37	36	46
Consortium	36	31	48	33	35	35	34	34	39
Balance of State	44	42	49	35	29	39	37	34	40

Source: Employment and Training Administration, U.S. Department of Labor (unpublished data).

[a]Job entry rates for Title II.

[b]Job entries as a percent of terminations, excluding those transferring to other CETA titles.

[c]Based on reports from 26 areas; 6 cities, 9 counties, 7 consortia, and 4 balance of states.

A special report by the House Committee on Government Operations summarized the problem (U.S. Congress, 1979a, p. 16):

> One critical weakness in all the reports is that they are not augmented by routine random checking of reported figures. DOL has very little ability to go behind the statistics. Specially directed investigations, for instance, have disclosed errors in the number of clients, the number of placements, and other key data.

JOB ENTRY RATES

Job entry rates for the first six months of 1979 were slightly higher than for the same period in 1978. When rates are examined by prime sponsor categories, cities are the only group that did not show an increase (Table 31). A previous NRC study showed lower job entry rates in 1976 and 1977 (National Research Council, 1978, p. 232). However, changes in the reporting requirements for intertitle transfers make year-to-year comparisons difficult. Prior to 1978, persons transferring from one title to another were counted as terminations. The effect of this was to understate the job entry ratio.

In fiscal 1978, indirect placements accounted for 52 percent of PSE placements, while self-placements were 47 percent of the total. In fiscal 1979, indirect placements increased to 59 percent, and self-placements fell to 40 percent of all PSE placements. Less than 1 percent of persons who obtain employment are direct placements.

The increase in the percentage of persons entering employment as a result of prime sponsor job development activities may be due to increased emphasis on transition prompted by the 18-month limit on participation. This effect may have been particularly important as large numbers of PSE workers reached the limit of their extended enrollment periods in the last month of fiscal 1979.

Success in placing participants who leave PSE programs may be influenced by a number of factors that are largely outside the control of the prime sponsor. Client characteristics and local economic conditions are two primary examples of such factors.

Client Characteristics

Department of Labor data for the third and fourth quarters of fiscal 1979 indicate that persons who are white, age 22-44, and have more than a high school education are the most likely to obtain unsubsidized employment immediately after they leave the PSE program (Figure 6 and Table 32). CLMS data on terminees who have been out of the program at least three

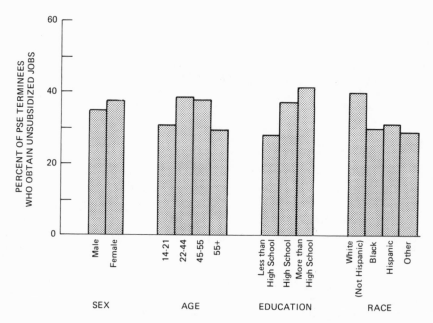

SOURCE: Based on Data from Employment and Training Administration

FIGURE 6   Job Entry Rates by Characteristics of CETA Public Service Employment Terminees, Third and Fourth Quarter, 1979

months support these findings. The CLMS data also suggest that males are more likely to find jobs than females, and that persons who are economically disadvantaged have lower job entry rates than those who are not (Westat, Inc., 1979, Table 17).

Based on our study sample, there appears to be a relationship between job entry and the participation of economically disadvantaged persons in PSE programs: the higher the relative percent of economically disadvantaged participants under a title, the lower the relative job entry rate. However, a relationship between other client characteristics and job entry could not be established.[2]

It is too early to make a conclusive statement about the impact of the tighter eligibility requirements of the reauthorization act on job entry rates. In the absence of countervailing initiatives to improve placements, however, it appears that job entry may be slightly constrained by the mandate to serve more economically disadvantaged persons.

TABLE 32 Job Entry Rates, Title IID and Title VI, by Selected
Characteristics of Terminees, April-September 1979

Participant Characteristics	Job Entry Rate[a]
TOTAL	36
Sex: Male	35
Female	37
Age: 21 and under	31
22-44	38
45-55	37
55 and over	29
Education:	
Less than High School	28
High School graduate or equivalent	37
Beyond High School	42
Economic Status:	
AFDC recipient	31
Economically disadvantaged	34
Race/Ethnic Group:	
White (not Hispanic)	40
Black (not Hispanic)	30
Hispanic	31
Other	29

Source: Data for persons terminating in quarters ending June 30, 1979 and September
30, 1979, based on Employment and Training Administration, U.S. Department of
Labor reports (unpublished).

[a]Job entries as a percent of terminations.

Local Employment Conditions

Contrary to expectations, there was no significant correlation between
unemployment rates and job entry rates. Areas in our sample with high
unemployment rates did not have significantly lower job entry rates than
areas with low unemployment rates.[3]

Moreover, year-to-year changes in job entry rates are not always
associated with similar changes in unemployment rates (Table 33).
Between 1978 and 1979, unemployment rates for the sponsors in our
sample declined by an average of 0.1 percentage point, while job entry
rates increased by 4 percentage points. This relationship is not consistent
among the sponsors, however. In cities, both the average job entry rate and
the average rate of unemployment declined; in counties, unemployment
declined, while job entry rates increased; in consortia, both the unemployment rate and the average job entry rate increased; and in balance-of-state

TABLE 33   Changes in CETA Public Service Employment Job Entry Rates and Changes in Unemployment Rates by Type of Prime Sponsor, Sample Prime Sponsor Areas, 1978-1979

Type of Prime Sponsor	Percentage Point Change in Job Entry Rate (January-June 1978 to January-June 1979) Total PSE	Percentage Point Change in Average Unemployment Rate (Calendar 1978 to January-June 1979)	Average Rate January-June 1979
ALL STUDY AREAS	+ 4	-0.1	6.1
City	- 8	-0.3	6.6
County	+10	-0.8	5.4
Consortium	+ 5	+1.2	5.7
Balance of State	+ 6	0.0	6.3

Source: Based on Employment and Training Administration and Bureau of Labor Statistics data, U.S. Department of Labor (unpublished) for 28 areas.

areas, the unemployment rate was unchanged, while the job entry rate increased.

LOCAL TRANSITION SYSTEMS

Local management policies could be the most significant factors affecting transition. Researchers have found only minor relationships between client characteristics, unemployment rates, and transition outcomes, but have suggested that variations in management policies could be important. A recent Ohio State University study of CETA management decisions and goal achievement indicated that differences in management can significantly affect placement results. The study concluded (Ohio State University, 1978, p. xiii):

The broadest finding is that management decisions at the local level have significant potential for improving program performance. By the same token, poor management has the potential for contributing to mediocre performance.

Although an attempt was made to relate current transition outcomes to variations in the management policies of the prime sponsors in our survey, available data from Employment and Training Administration's (ETA) Management Information System on job entry rates were judged to be inadequate for this purpose. Although the data may be sufficiently accurate to be used as performance indicators for a large sample, errors in the data became important when the data were used as performance indicators for the sponsors in our study. We have not, therefore, included an empirical analysis of the variations in job entry rates as they relate to differences in management among the sponsors in our study.

PLANNING FOR TRANSITION

Under the reauthorization act and accompanying regulations, plans must contain three elements that are prerequisites for a successful transition program:

- An analysis of the local labor market that identifies the local industries and occupations with growth potential;
- A strategy for training and placing participants in such jobs; and
- Realistic placement goals based upon the supply of jobs and the needs and capabilities of the program participants.

More often than not, however, placement strategies are not based upon an analysis of the labor market conditions, and transition goals are not set forth as part of the transition strategy.

Labor Market Analysis

Two-thirds of the sponsors in our sample reported that preparation of the labor market analysis was one of the most difficult tasks in the planning process. Only 25 percent included an analysis of prospective job openings in specific occupations in their plans for transition. Although such analyses are periodically available from the employment service, the geographic areas used in these analyses may not conform to the geographic configuration of the prime sponsor jurisdiction. Furthermore, the analyses of the employment service are generally not up-to-date, and details needed for transition planning are missing.

A labor market analysis that identified growth industries and occupations would be useful in planning for both PSE positions and training. The Department of Labor assumes that the information needed for such an analysis is readily available. The 1979 Department of Labor's *Forms Preparation Handbook* suggests that employment service reports be used to describe the industrial and occupational composition of the local labor market and instructs the sponsor to "indicate (1) the current demand for labor as well as the estimated demand, if known, for the next five years, and (2) the availability of pre-employment and post-employment training for local residents funded from sources other than CETA. . . . " But there is inadequate guidance on how to project labor market needs based on the potential growth of the product market, labor turnover rates, population trends, or the numerous other factors that may affect the demand and supply of workers in a particular industry or occupation.

Transition Strategies

The requirement to include a transition strategy in the annual plan was met by about 60 percent of the prime sponsors. The strategies are based on three approaches: (1) job development by CETA staff or delegated agencies; (2) job search by the PSE participant; and (3) skill training.

When all of the sample sponsors were questioned about their transition strategy, about 40 percent said they rely primarily on job developers to open opportunities for PSE participants in unsubsidized employment. Another 40 percent emphasize job search activities by the participants, and the remainder stress skill training.

A lack of emphasis on skill training was also noted in a recent study by the University of Texas. The report concluded (University of Texas at Austin, 1978, p. 23):

Skill training was the least emphasized means of enhancing employability in public service employment. In the eight Texas sites, PSE participants generally received little skill development training transferable to the private sector. There were no assurances asked for or required by CETA program staff that training and skill development received would be adequate to prepare participants for unsubsidized jobs.

Sponsors who include an analysis of the local labor market with respect to prospective jobs in specific occupations in their plan tend to use this information to develop unsubsidized job opportunities for participants; those who do not tend to leave the problem of finding employment to the participant (Table 34). None of the sponsors who studied the job market emphasized participant job search as a transition strategy.

Since Title IID is aimed primarily at the structurally unemployed, one would expect more emphasis on skill training for Title IID participants than for Title VI enrollees. In our study, only two sponsors emphasized skill training for Title IID enrollees but not for Title VI participants. This is consistent with evidence indicating that the characteristics of the participants under the two titles are becoming more alike (see Chapter 3).

Prime sponsors and field associates overwhelmingly believe job development to be the most effective course of action. In areas that emphasize job development, 80 percent of the field associates and 60 percent of the sponsors reported that the strategy is effective. In contrast, none of the

TABLE 34 Public Service Employment Transition Strategies, by Use of Labor Market Analysis of Job Openings in Specific Occupations, Sample Prime Sponsor Areas (percent of sponsors)

Major Transition Strategy	Title IID			Title VI		
	Total	Labor Market Analysis	No Labor Market Analysis	Total	Labor Market Analysis	No Labor Market Analysis
TOTAL	100	100	100	100	100	100
Job Development	40	71	28	44	86	28
Job Search by Participant	40	0	56	44	0	62
Skill Training	20	29	17	12	14	11

Source: Based on reports from 25 areas.

NOTE: Details may not add to totals due to rounding.

sponsors and only 10 percent of the field representatives in areas that rely on participant job search believe that their approach is effective.

Setting Goals

Despite the legislative requirement to establish quantitative transition goals, only 40 percent of the sponsors in the sample had cited numerical transition goals as part of their transition strategy.

Very few sponsors set different goals for Titles IID and VI. Where the goals differed, however, Title IID targets were higher. This suggests that goals may be based more on past experience than on expected differences in the populations. In 1978, prior to the reauthorization act, Title II PSE programs included a greater share of highly qualified participants, and placement rates were higher for Title II PSE participants. As these participants leave the program and are replaced by persons subject to the new eligibility provisions, sponsors may revise their goals to reflect the new participant populations.

Prime sponsors who considered their transition strategy effective were more inclined to set goals than those who viewed the strategy as ineffective. One-half of the former group set targets for themselves; only one-quarter of the latter group did so.

The goals set for transition varied widely. Title IID goals ranged from 11 percent of terminations to 85 percent, and averaged about 45 percent. In Title VI, the average goal was about 41 percent, but the range was from 29 to 85 percent. In general, higher placement goals were set by prime sponsors who had done a labor market analysis and emphasized job development as a transition strategy.

ORGANIZATION AND MANAGEMENT

The emphasis placed on transition and the ways in which sponsors manage the placement activity vary considerably.

Location of the Placement Function

Approximately 40 percent of the sponsors in our sample handled the placement function primarily within their own organization. About 25 percent delegate the function to the employment service, 11 percent rely on program agents, and another 25 percent assign it to program operators, employers, or outside contractors. The 40 percent who have retained the placement function generally use a central placement unit that serves all CETA participants. When placements are made by program agents, program operators, or outside contractors, PSE workers are likely to be handled separately from other CETA clients.

Because of the decentralized nature of the balance-of-state operations, none of these sponsors in our sample undertake the placement functions themselves (Table 35). They rely primarily upon the employment service. Cities and counties, on the other hand, are most likely to keep the placement function in-house. Consortia made extensive use of program operators and PSE employers, but also relied heavily upon their own organization.

Employability Development Plans (EDP)

Title IID has been designed as a program for persons with severe employment handicaps. To ensure that the special needs of these participants are accommodated, the act requires that prime sponsors prepare individual plans that identify the employability needs of each participant and indicate the services to be provided and the plan to secure unsubsidized employment upon completion of the program (see Appendix C). Ninety percent of the prime sponsors say they also plan to prepare EDPs for Title VI participants.

Sponsors differ widely in their view of EDPs and the manner in which

TABLE 35 Location of Primary Responsibility for Public Service Employment Placement Function, by Type of Prime Sponsor, Sample Prime Sponsor
Areas (percentage distribution)

Location of Placement Function	Total (N = 28)	Cities (N = 6)	Counties (N = 9)	Consortia (N = 9)	Balance of States (N = 4)
TOTAL	100	100	100	100	100
CETA Administration	39	50	56	33	0
Program Agent	11	0	0	22	25
Employment Service	25	17	33	11	50
Program Operators, Employers, Subcontractors	25	33	11	33	25

NOTE: Details may not add to totals due to rounding.

they implement them. Most sponsors prepare EDPs before the participant
is enrolled and assigned to a program. In 37 percent of the sample areas,
however, the EDPs are written after enrollment. In these instances, the
plans simply record decisions that have already been made.

In about half of the prime sponsor areas, the EDP process includes a
counseling interview to assess aptitude and interest. Quarterly follow-up
interviews with participants have been planned to ensure that the goals of
the EDP are being met by the PSE job and supportive services and to
make any necessary changes in the participants' EDP. Contact with
employers to check on employee progress is generally included as part of
the process. Thus far, not many of these follow-up interviews have been
conducted. In some instances, sponsors plan to limit the follow-ups to a
telephone check once a year. In spite of the requirement of the law,
sponsors in 15 percent of the areas do not plan to do any follow-ups at all.

About half of the sponsors in our sample consider the EDP program
worthwhile. Forty percent regard them as a paper exercise, and 10 percent
are not yet certain of their value. The usefulness of an EDP depends upon
the attitudes, motivation, and abilities of the sponsor, the employer, and
the participant. One respondent noted:

It's not the EDP document—it's the act of interviewing and asking questions of the
enrollee, and then following up. This tells the participant that the PSE job is not an
end in itself but is intended to lead to something else for which the participant has
indicated a preference.

Three-quarters of the sponsors who regard EDPs as worthwhile prepare them prior to enrollment, and most have already begun tracking the participants. In contrast, a majority of the sponsors who think EDPs are not worth the effort write them after enrollment, and only one has conducted any follow-up.

The reaction of a prime sponsor to EDPs as a transition device is closely associated with the sponsor's use of other transition tools. Prime sponsors who tend to do more thorough planning for transition and emphasize job development also tend to view employability development plans as a useful tool to promote transition.

The importance of adequate numbers of competent staff members and the need for staff training were stressed by many of our research associates. One associate commented:

EDPs are an indispensable part of manpower training and development but they place a heavy burden on the skills and judgment of the CETA staff. Until they are trained in some way . . . it is a pro forma procedure that induces cynicism in those who are asked to do it but are not sure that they are doing anything that is meaningful.

An average caseload of 60 clients per counselor would require about 5,000 employability development specialists to serve the PSE population, or an average of about 10 counselors per sponsor. While some currently employed counselors are certainly capable of providing the necessary services, there is a need for more trained staff in this area.

Other Policies to Promote Transition

Although not specifically required by the reauthorization act, some sponsors have adopted two additional policies to improve transition opportunities. One of these policies requires PSE workers to register with and actively seek employment through the Employment Service for the duration of their stay in PSE. The other establishes placement goals for individual employers and makes their continued participation in PSE contingent upon an acceptable placement record.

Requiring participants to actively pursue unsubsidized jobs through the Employment Service not only serves to remind the workers that PSE is not permanent employment, but also increases their job market exposure at little, if any, additional cost to the prime sponsor. Two-thirds of the sponsors require PSE participants to register with the ES and remain active job seekers.

Sponsors are required to consider "demonstrated effectiveness" when selecting PSE employers. Our survey found, however, that less than 30 percent had established placement goals for PSE employers and only 18 percent had ever eliminated a PSE employer from the program because of poor placement performance. The fact that only one sponsor relied, as a primary transition strategy, on the transfer of PSE participants into regular jobs with their PSE employers suggests that very little pressure is being put on PSE employers to find permanent positions in their own organizations for PSE workers.

Merit Systems and Unions

The transition of PSE participants into regular public sector jobs was not significantly affected by merit hiring systems or employee organizations.

About 75 percent of the sponsors in our sample reported that the largest PSE employer in their jurisdiction operated under a merit hiring system. These areas had an average job entry rate of 36 percent, almost 10 percentage points lower than those without such systems.

Two-thirds of the prime sponsors reported that some PSE employees in their jurisdiction are covered by a collective bargaining agreement. In these areas, an average of about 25 percent of the PSE workers are subject to a union agreement. Less than 20 percent of the agreements, however, specifically address the issue of moving PSE workers into regular unsubsidized jobs.

None of the agreements that do cover transition permit employers to limit vacant positions above entry level to PSE workers. There are no limits, however, on the types of jobs for which former PSE workers can be hired.

Six prime sponsors reported union-related problems involving transition issues. For the most part, however, they were personal grievances or other minor problems. Sixty percent of the field research associates reported that unions were neutral in their attitude toward PSE transition. None believed that the unions resist the transfer of PSE workers to unsubsidized jobs, and 30 percent reported that the unions encouraged such transition.

SUMMARY

The reauthorization act attempted to revitalize the transition objectives of the PSE program. A slight increase in placement rates has occurred since the act took effect. The 18-month limit on the duration of PSE employment has generated pressure on participants to seek unsubsidized job opportunities and on employers to provide permanent positions for enrollees whose terms have come to end. It is, however, too early to assess the impact on transition of other reauthorization provisions such as the stricter eligibility requirements.

Some prime sponsors have developed intensive job placement systems to assist PSE participants in finding unsubsidized employment, and consider employability development plans and job development services integral parts of their programs. However, widespread weaknesses in the transition processes have been noted.

• Transition planning is inadequate in most jurisdictions. Sponsors generally do not have the labor market information necessary to direct PSE participants to job opportunities in industries and occupations with growth potential.

• Many sponsors do not have enough adequately trained staff to prepare meaningful employability development plans; nor do they have access to technical assistance and training resources in this area. Hence, in many jurisdictions, EDPs have become merely a formality.

• Placement data are inadequate to assess the effectiveness of programs and are not reported in a consistent manner by prime sponsors.

NOTES

1. Prior to 1979, a person who entered the armed forces was recorded under "other positive termination."

2. Similar results were reported in Ohio State Uniersity (1978, p. 92).

3. See also National Research Council (1978, p. 229); Ohio State University (1978, p. 82); and University of Texas at Austin (1978, p. 54).

6 Program Monitoring

The integrity of CETA public service employment programs was seriously questioned during the debate on the reauthorization bill in 1978. The criticism came from several directions. The media highlighted "horror" stories of fraud and abuse. Congressional mail described abuses in local programs. The Government Accounting Office reported that CETA suffered from inadequate staff and ineffective monitoring procedures. Even an audit by the Department of Labor (DOL) indicated that 1 in every 10 enrollees in Title VI did not meet the eligibility criteria.

Several factors contributed to this state of affairs, but the most important were the emphasis on a rapid increase in enrollment in response to the economic stimulus program of 1977, the inadequacy of monitoring by both prime sponsors and the Department of Labor, and the failure on the part of Congress to explicitly address the assignment of liability or the imposition of sanctions in the event of improper enrollment of PSE participants.

The effect of the pressure on prime sponsors to increase PSE enrollment from 300,000 in May 1977 to 725,000 by March 1978 was noted by Congressman Ronald A. Sarasin in August 1978 (*Congressional Record*, 1978a, p. H8164):

No system of management could have survived this rapid increase without some fraud, some abuse, and some terrible cases of mismanagement. Indeed, it is something of a minor miracle that there were not more problems than we have already witnessed.

121

The attempts to characterize the entire CETA program on the basis of selected incidents were resented by program managers. However, it was apparent that program monitoring was weak, accountability was lacking, and the eligibility of participants was not adequately verified.

This chapter identifies the actions taken by Congress and DOL to eliminate program abuse, describes their implementation, and assesses their effects.

CONGRESSIONAL ACTIONS

To ensure better management and continued acceptance of the Public Service Employment (PSE) program by the public, Congress used the occasion of the CETA reauthorization to prevent further abuses:

- It required all prime sponsors to establish an independent unit "to monitor compliance with the requirements of CETA";
- It required prime sponsors to install a "proven method" for verifying participant eligibility;
- It defined the liability of the prime sponsor for the enrollment of ineligible participants;
- It clarified the investigative responsibilities of various levels of administration; and
- It called for the establishment of an Office of Management Assistance in the Department of Labor to aid prime sponsors in both solving program problems and complying with the requirements of the new legislation.

INDEPENDENT MONITORING UNITS

The requirement that prime sponsors establish an independent monitoring unit (IMU) was expected to strengthen the stewardship of the CETA program. Although the requirement was triggered by instances of fraud and abuse, the mandate was a broad one and included program review as well. The IMU was to "monitor compliance with the requirements of this Act, the regulations issued thereunder, and the comprehensive employment and training plan" (Title I, Sect. 121(q)). The implementing regulations issued by the Department of Labor emphasized the comprehensiveness of the review responsibilities assigned to the IMU. They called for periodic monitoring and review of all program activities through on-site visits and examination of program data.

As of September 1, 1979, five months after the IMUs should have been in operation, 25 percent of the sponsors in our survey had not yet established such units. The IMUs that had been established at the time of our interviews (June-July 1979) had had little time to function under the new requirements. As a result, much of the information on IMUs reflects plans and expectations, rather than operating experience.

Under the DOL regulations, prime sponsors were authorized to require program agents and other subrecipients to establish independent monitoring units whenever "administratively feasible." However, none of the consortium or balance-of-state prime sponsors in the study had required any program agents to set up IMUs, and only one sponsor had required a subrecipient to establish an IMU. Most sponsors reported that their program agents and subrecipients do some monitoring, but in most instances the monitoring has not changed since the reauthorization.

INDEPENDENCE AND AUTHORITY

The effectiveness of the IMUs depends in part on the degree of their independence and the range of their activities. These issues, however, have been a continuous source of confusion.

The implications of the term "independent" have drawn considerable attention. The April 3, 1979, regulations stipulated that the IMU be a "part of internal program management" and that it be independent of and not accountable to any unit being monitored, and suggested that it report to the CETA director or the chief elected official in the district. Nonetheless, some regional offices, concerned with the degree of independence possible under this system, gave only tentative approval to monitoring units that reported to the CETA director, pending further interpretation of the directive. An October 10, 1979, ETA field memorandum repeated the suggestion that the IMU report to the CETA director or chief elected official. Although this would appear to settle the question of the organizational location of the IMU, some confusion still exists. The field memo has been interpreted by some to mean that the units should be separate entities "outside the prime sponsor."

An attempt by the Department of Labor to define the permissible activities of the IMU also resulted in confusion. A preliminary field memo prepared in June 1979 would have precluded the use of IMUs to perform the participant-eligibility reviews that are required by the law and that must be conducted within 30 days of enrollment. The memo further stated that IMUs could not be "in charge of, or a part of the Equal Employment Opportunity (EEO) unit." This draft was widely circulated through informal channels, and many sponsors, assuming that its provisions would be imposed, organized their units to conform to it. The final version, released four months later, reversed these policies, and currently, IMUs are used for these purposes.

In our survey, approximately 90 percent of the IMU heads were appointed by the CETA administrators and reported to them. The CETA director generally defined the scope of the IMU's activities and the disposition of its findings. In most cases, the director granted the IMU a large degree of freedom. One field representative noted that the support of the CETA director had assured independent action by the IMU. "The key thing," he said, "is that the administrator is interested in giving the IMU a large measure of independence."

In some instances, however, the CETA director has seriously limited the authority of the IMU. Two sponsors, for example, did not permit the IMU to choose the subject matter to be reviewed. The attitude of one sponsor was described in these terms:

The sponsor seems to consider the establishment of the unit merely a formality; he does not seem to be concerned with the issue of its powers. It is also worth noting that the head of the unit has still not been appointed, so that control is remaining with the administrator as long as possible.

All of the IMUs had the authority to review any pertinent records and to interview appropriate individuals. At the time of our study, about two-thirds of the units had exercised this authority. Similarly, all of the units were permitted to visit work sites without advance notice, although less than half had done so. However, four out of five IMUs were not permitted to issue reports to outside persons without specific approval of the CETA administrator or chief elected official. In five areas, the IMUs may issue reports without obtaining approval, but none had done so.

On balance, the creation of IMUs has served to highlight the monitoring issue and has given the activity greater status and visibility.

STAFFING

Sponsors reported that the number of personnel engaged in monitoring and evaluation was slightly larger than the number of personnel assigned to IMUs; these figures suggest that some program review activities were performed by persons outside of the IMUs (see Chapter 2). The newly designated IMUs accounted for an average of five full-time monitoring and evaluation positions in 1979.

Although the resources devoted to the activity have increased only modestly, monitoring is now likely to be more centralized and systematized than previously. Prior to 1979, a number of areas had either no separately identified monitoring staff, or a small separate staff that worked in conjunction with some part-time monitoring and program review employees who were assigned to program implementation and operation units.

According to the field study, most IMUs consisted of an administrator, one or two investigators, program specialists, and a clerk. Seventeen of the twenty-four prime sponsors that reported staffing patterns had no internal auditors. Financial auditing is often the responsibility of personnel outside the CETA staff. Units that employed auditors had an average of three.

Field associates for the study reported wide variations in the quality of the personnel assigned to IMUs. Most said that the IMUs were staffed with competent individuals. A few indicated that the staffs lacked accounting and investigative skills, and one wrote that the IMU was a dumping ground for staff deadwood.

IMU responsibilities require specialists in a large number of program areas. Recruiting such personnel is difficult. One field associate presented the problem in these terms:

Much depends on the IMU. [The staff members must be] financial wizards, with the ability to study internal systems and suggest corrective steps and study program operations in the field and make suggestions—a tall order. . . . So much depends on a knowledgeable and competent staff. But they are sadly in short supply.

MONITORING ACTIVITIES

The emphasis on monitoring in the 1978 legislation was expected to result in more intensive and comprehensive efforts in about 90 percent of the study areas. About 60 percent of the prime sponsors indicated that their monitoring activities were fairly evenly divided between improving program quality and preventing fraud and abuse. Almost a third concentrated primarily on program quality, and about 10 percent focused mainly on fraud and abuse.

In over 80 percent of the areas there will be increased monitoring to check that CETA actually fulfills its mission to assist enrollees in obtaining unsubsidized jobs. Over three-fourths of the study areas also expect to increase the monitoring of participant eligibility and enrollee wages— subjects given special attention in the 1978 legislation.

Maintenance of effort, which refers to the CETA requirement that public service employment not result in a reduction in the number of regular positions that would be filled normally, was a major concern of Congress in the 1976 CETA amendments. It was monitored in almost all areas before the 1978 reauthorization and has received relatively little additional attention since that time (Table 36).

TABLE 36   Activities Monitored Before and After the CETA Reauthorization, Sample Prime Sponsor Areas (percent of areas)

Type of Activity	Monitored Prior to the Reauthorization	Monitored After the Reauthorization	Increased Monitoring Activity After the Reauthorization[a]
PROGRAM QUALITY			
Assistance in transfer of enrollees to unsubsidized jobs	83	100	83
Enrollee training	74	83	70
Enrolling the most disadvantaged	61	74	57
Supervision of enrollees	87	91	43
LEGAL REQUIREMENTS			
Eligibility of participants	74	96	78
Wages and wage supplementation	70	83	78
Fraud	74	83	74
Handling of CETA funds	87	96	61
Pay records	87	100	52
Maintenance of effort	96	96	43
Attendance of enrollees	96	100	35

Source: Based on reports from 28 areas.

[a]Represents the percent of prime sponsors who reported either new monitoring activity or increased monitoring activity after reauthorization.

Sponsors reported that verification of the eligibility of applicants for CETA programs is a major activity of the monitoring units. In one area, the field associate observed,

Client eligibility verification and the collection of information to document client eligibility seems to be getting the most attention. One result will probably be a smaller proportion of ineligible clients. However, the trade-off may be that program quality and overall program management will receive too little attention.

Eligibility verification, which will be discussed in greater detail later in this chapter, is difficult because it depends to a great extent on the information provided by the applicants. Prime sponsors are faced with the almost impossible task of judging whether applicants misstate information about family income or previous employment.

Monitoring maintenance of effort also poses problems for sponsors because determinations must be made about the activities that agencies would have supported with their regular budgets in the absence of CETA. In the words of one sponsor, "it is easy to conceal violations behind bureaucratic rhetoric and political maneuvers." Moreover, there is no uniform definition of substitution, nor are there guidelines to identify the various forms it may take.

Sponsors generally expressed a need for more guidance from the national office as to what constitutes fraudulent activity. One sponsor pointed out that, "There is a fine line between merely being out of compliance and actual intentional fraudulent activity, especially with new agencies which are unfamiliar with CETA." Another sponsor reported,

[We have difficulty] knowing where to draw the line—whether to turn over a case to the Inspector General or to local authorities. There seems to be no solid basis for making such distinctions.

It had been presumed that the increased use of nonprofit organizations would increase the monitoring burden on prime sponsors. The evidence, however, is equivocal. The survey data indicate that sponsors are evenly divided on the question of whether it is more difficult to monitor nonprofit organizations or government agencies. Some sponsors maintain that nonprofit organizations are more difficult to monitor because their record-keeping ability is inferior; others, however, feel that nonprofit organizations are more cooperative and easier to monitor because their projects are smaller.

MONITORING RESULTS

As previously noted, IMUs had done only a small amount of monitoring at the time of our interviews. Thus, most of the responses concerning the effects of the new monitoring efforts were based more on expectations than on experience. About a third of the sponsors in the study sample thought that more time was needed before they could predict the results of their monitoring. Of sponsors willing to make predictions, the number who believed that monitoring would reduce fraud and abuse exceeded the number that did not. For the other monitoring categories, the number of sponsors expecting improvement was smaller than the number of sponsors who expected no change (Table 37).

TABLE 37   Local Officials' Perceptions of Anticipated Effects of New
Monitoring Efforts, Sample Prime Sponsor Areas (percent of areas)

Monitoring Categories	Expect Improvement	Expect No Change	Don't Know
Deter fraud and abuse	41	30	30
Employer performance	30	41	30
Service to disadvantaged	22	48	30
Performance of participants	15	48	37
Transition	11	59	30
Usefulness of services	11	56	33

Source: Based on reports from 27 areas.

NOTE: Details may not add to 100 percent due to rounding.

Half of the sponsors reported that formal allegations of fraud or abuse
had been made in their jurisdictions in the last two years. These sponsors,
however, did not differ in their expectations for improvement from
sponsors who had not been confronted with allegations. Nor was there any
difference between the two groups of sponsors with respect to the type of
monitoring that they perform, i.e., on-site monitoring or desk audits.

Several CETA administrators, who bear the responsibility for adminis-
trating IMUs and who must face the consequences of adverse findings,
questioned the value of the increased emphasis on monitoring. They are
concerned that the negative impact of the IMUs will outweigh any benefits
that may accrue. The observations of some field associates reflect this
feeling.

[The prime sponsor] feels that monitoring had been conducted adequately in the
past and the IMU just adds an additional layer in his administration. He also feels
that the existence of the IMU will generate more meaningless complaints from
subgrantees and clients than in the past. . . .

The more intensive monitoring has probably been harmful in a minor way,
because resources are diverted from more beneficial activities—additional enrollment and use of staff for counseling and development of training. . . .

CETA at the local level is already overcontrolled and runs the great risk of
strangulation if this doesn't ease up. Staff turnover is reaching alarming
proportions, and the "chilling effect" of more and more controls can only be a
further stifling of local initiative.

ELIGIBILITY VERIFICATION AND LIABILITY FOR INELIGIBLE PARTICIPANTS

The financial and criminal liability penalties for enrolling ineligible persons in CETA programs have had a profound effect on the procedures used to verify the eligibility of participants. Although the verification requirements in the law and regulations are specific and extensive, many prime sponsors have gone even further to reduce their vulnerability.

The regulations prescribe four steps for determining and verifying eligibility (Sect. 676.75-3). The process begins with the completion of an application form designed to provide the information necessary to determine eligibility. The applicant is required to certify that the information provided is true. The specific elements of the application form are listed in the regulations, and a sample is included in the 1979 *Forms Preparation Handbook for FY 1980*, issued by the U.S. Department of Labor (1979a). The second step is the determination of eligibility based on the information on the application. This determination may be made by the sponsor, a subgrantee, or a delegated agency. The applicant may be enrolled immediately upon this finding. Within 30 days after enrollment, the reauthorization act requires a desk review of the application. Finally, on a quarterly basis, sponsors must take a random sample of new enrollees and verify the accuracy of the information provided on the application forms. Among the items that must be verified are residence, family income, family size, public assistance status, labor force status, prior CETA participation, and school enrollment. Verification may consist of documentary evidence (driver's license, tax forms, insurance papers) or, when documents are not available, confirmation by a third party.

The regulations do not require documentation of the items on the application form at the time it is submitted, and initial eligibility can be determined solely on the basis of the information provided on the application. In practice, however, applicants are generally required to document income, unemployment insurance (UI) status, social security number, welfare status, and residence before a determination of eligibility is made. Over 80 percent of the sponsors report that they verify this and other information prior to the 30-day desk audit.

Documentation of application form items is not required for the 30-day review either, unless an inconsistency is discovered during the process. Again, however, the majority of prime sponsors make telephone checks with previous employers and assemble other collateral evidence of nearly all items used for eligibility determination. Thus, many sponsors completely verify the eligibility of all enrollees. Although the desk audit need not be performed prior to enrollment, almost half of the prime sponsors will not enroll participants until the audit has been completed. To protect themselves, sponsors are "making sure, doubly sure."

When the required quarterly sample of new enrollees is verified, very few sponsors need do anything more than review the documentation already in the participants' files. One prime sponsor viewed the sample verification as "overkill" and decided not to do it at all. The field associate for the area noted,

During the desk audit they identify errors and correct them by gathering more information and resolving differences. If major errors are found . . . procedures call for verification. This may mean *some* or *all* of the information on the application. They estimate that, using this approach, they are in fact verifying 18 percent of all applicants and are not drawing a quarterly sample.

LIABILITY FOR INELIGIBLE PARTICIPANTS

Prior to the reauthorization act, CETA did not specify that sponsors were liable for the costs of employing ineligible participants. To facilitate the rapid buildup of Title VI and to enhance the role of employment service offices, prime sponsors were encouraged to enter into agreements that assigned responsibility for eligibility certification to state employment security agencies. About 60 percent of the sponsors in our sample had such agreements in fiscal 1978. Where such arrangements were made, neither the employment service nor the prime sponsor was liable for the costs resulting from ineligible enrollments. Employment and Training Administration (ETA) Field Memorandum 421-78 of August 1978 spelled out the departmental policy:

If income and residence are also verified under agreements with the SESA/welfare agency, current regulations are interpreted that neither the prime sponsor nor the SESA/welfare agency will be held liable for payments to ineligible participants.

To remedy this "no fault" ineligibility policy, Congress made prime sponsors liable for the costs of ineligible enrollments, but permitted determination of eligibility to be delegated with the approval of the secretary and with reasonable safeguards and provisions for "reimbursement of costs because of erroneous decisions made with insufficient care" by the delegated agency. The regulations added, "where funds cannot be recovered, the prime sponsor is responsible for such liabilities." This language, however, left two questions unanswered: (1) What constitutes sufficient care? (2) Under what circumstances will the delegated agency have the funds to repay money misspent on ineligibles?

An Employment and Training Administration policy clarification of

February 1979 attempted to resolve the uncertainty by ruling that, "The grant officer may allow costs if the system was good, effectively implemented, and the total costs will not be too great." But this formulation, too, raised as many questions as it answered. The operative elements of the criteria—"good," "effectively implemented," and "too great"—were left undefined. At this point in time, it is impossible to know how the policies will be interpreted and applied.

In addition to establishing financial liability, the reauthorization act makes it a criminal offense to knowingly hire ineligible persons for CETA positions. Because this provision poses a direct personal threat to individuals responsible for hiring, it may have a greater effect on the program than the financial liability provisions.

The determination and verification systems now employed go far beyond procedures required by the reauthorization act or the Department of Labor. These systems reflect the concern of sponsors about the liability provisions of the act. Our survey revealed a surprising amount of confusion about these provisions.

Although most respondents believe that the ultimate responsibility lies with the prime sponsor, some believe that the employment service or program agents will be liable, and a few do not know who is liable (Table 38). Several sponsors recognized that regional and local officials were not operating under the same liability assumptions and thought the problem occurred because the Department of Labor had not provided adequate guidelines.

Initially, these uncertainties led prime sponsors to develop verification systems that exceeded the requirements. A continuation of this vagueness may have the reverse effect. At this point, no one is sure under what circumstances liability will be imposed or who will be held liable. To many, it appears that the department does not plan to enforce the liability provisions at all. Already, some sponsors have cut back on their original verification efforts. According to one field associate,

The employment service and prime sponsor have had problems interpreting the regulations and getting systems in place. First, the prime sponsor required that everything be done on every applicant. Now, after things have relaxed, the employment service desk review is used as a signal to verify.

Another field associate observed that, "The new financial liability provision does not seem to concern the prime too much; perhaps because he assumes that this provision is unlikely to actually be enforced."

Many respondents feel that the longer the department waits to begin monitoring and enforcing these provisions, the more likely it is that this

TABLE 38   Perceptions of Liability (percent of respondents)

Respondent	Agency Which is Liable			
	Prime Sponsor	Employment Service	Other (Program Agents, Contractor)	Don't Know
Prime sponsor[a]	75	11	11	4
Employment service[b]	61	9	17	13
Regional office[c]	88	4	4	4

[a]Based on 28 respondents.
[b]Based on 23 respondents.
[c]Based on 25 respondents.

NOTE: Details may not add to 100 percent due to rounding.

attitude will spread. One respondent concluded that, "A few cases will have to be processed before one will really know who produces the cash." If none are processed, sponsors may conclude that the delays, burdensome processes, and costs involved with verification are not worth the trouble.

DELEGATION OF THE VERIFICATION FUNCTION

Prime sponsors were reluctant to delegate responsibility for eligibility verification because of the liability they might face. As Table 39 indicates, they were less likely to delegate responsibility for the desk review than for the initial determination of eligibility; they were least likely to delegate responsibility for the quarterly sample verifications. The closer the eligibility check was to a final review, the more likely the prime sponsor was to perform the check in-house. Almost invariably, sponsors attributed this practice to their reluctance to accept liability for someone else's mistakes. As one associate put it, "They trust themselves."

PROCEDURAL CHANGES

Although many sponsors report that they have always followed procedures similar to those required by the reauthorization act, the eligibility verification processes generally have become more rigorous. Over 70 percent of the sponsors reported that they had previously performed desk checks, and 85 percent reported that the organization that performed the reviews had not changed. Some verification similar to the required

TABLE 39 Assignment of Eligibility Determination and Verification Functions, Sample Prime Sponsor Areas (percent of sponsors)

Organization	Initial Determination	Desk Audit	Sample Verification
CETA administration	27	65	92
Employment service	69	19	4
Other agency (Program agent or subcontractor)	4	15	4

NOTE: Details may not add to 100 percent due to rounding.

quarterly sample had been done in about 40 percent of the sponsor areas, although not as frequently or as systematically as is now required. Even among the sponsors who reported that they always had an intensive verification system, however, there is agreement that current procedures are more rigorous. As one sponsor noted, "The process of verifying eligiblity is essentially the same, although consistency is checked more frequently and documentation is asked for more often."

There are some areas, though, that required no documentation of eligibility before the reauthorization act. Documentation requirements have increased in these and other areas since the act was passed. As examples of the more thorough procedures that have been required, one sponsor cited contacts with previous employers and written documentation by the welfare and UI offices of transfer payments. Another sponsor noted that they had never before requested wage stubs or tax records to prove income.

VERIFICATION PROBLEMS

Nearly every item that requires documentation can present a problem. The most difficult items to verify, according to sponsors in the study, are family status, date of last employment, and nepotism. It is usually difficult to prove that an applicant deliberately lied. One field research associate explained,

People don't always have the necessary documentation—they don't pay taxes, or drive, etc. Problems of nepotism are almost impossible to prevent, except through some quirk, especially if the deception is deliberate.

Information can be obtained by visiting homes and phoning neighbors, but sponsors are reluctant to engage in this kind of prying. There is growing concern for the privacy of clients, and a feeling that surveillance might become excessive. Said one respondent, with resignation, "Some things just can't be verified, short of sending a policeman into the home unannounced."

Some of these problems have been anticipated by the Department of Labor. The *Forms Preparation Handbook* allows sponsors to use "collateral contacts"—verbal confirmation of items by a third party—where written documentation is not available.

IMPACT ON PROGRAM OPERATIONS

The new verification requirements and the sanctions contained in the reauthorization act have significantly affected program operations.

More than half of the sponsors reported that more time was needed to enroll participants after the act than before. Delays of three days to three weeks were cited, and clients sometimes must make two visits in order to provide the missing documentation. In one area, the application must be approved by four separate individuals before enrollment. A typical field associate report stated,

The prime sponsor, thinking it could save time during the quarterly sample, has elected to do elaborate verification before enrollment. This has created a bottleneck. Lag times up to several weeks occur.

Prime sponsors generally take a dim view of these delays because they do not believe that the new procedures significantly reduce the number of ineligibles. Nor do they believe that many ineligibles slipped through their previous verification systems. They have instituted complex and time-consuming requirements only because they fear the personal and financial liability attached to the admission of ineligible participants. "More paperwork is undertaken," noted one field associate, "not to improve the program, but to protect the consortium."

Documentation requirements also intimidate some potential participants. In the view of some sponsors, requests for such detailed information reflect an assumption that the applicant is dishonest. Applicants, many of whom are eligible, sometimes refuse to provide the required documents or simply do not have them, and therefore drop out of the system. Concern was expressed by several prime sponsors that the people who drop out may be those most in need.

Some sponsors believe that the new wage and job tenure limits are themselves screening devices that make detailed documentation less necessary. In their view, applicants are not likely to misrepresent their situations to obtain low-paying, short-duration jobs. One respondent characterized the process as "asking applicants to provide life histories for $2.90 an hour." The underlying feeling seems to be that if the applicant is willing to work under those conditions, he probably needs the job.

Three sponsors thought that enrollment levels were currently constrained by the new verification process, and several more speculated that future PSE buildup could be hindered. These constraints could have serious implications if an expansion of the PSE program was needed to meet countercyclical objectives or to accommodate the jobs portion of the proposed welfare reform legislation.

Two sponsors reported that program agents in their jurisdictions had withdrawn from the program specifically because of the new eligibility verification provisions. In one of these areas, the program agent felt that the liability to which it was subject was not worth the benefits that might be derived from the program. In the other case, the program agents felt that the paperwork involved in the verification system had added so much administrative overhead that they could no longer function effectively.

Although everyone agrees that accountability is desirable and that fraud and abuse should not be tolerated, there is concern that too much is now expected. Said one respondent, "The idea of a 'zero-defect' program in the social service field may not be too realistic."

FEDERAL RESPONSIBILITIES AND ACTIVITIES

In addition to tightening monitoring procedures at the local level, the reauthorization act also prescribed actions to be taken by the Department of Labor. The secretary of labor is authorized (Sect. 133) to conduct any investigation necessary to determine whether provisions of the act or the regulations have been violated, and is further directed to provide for the continuing evaluation of all activities conducted pursuant to the act.

Federal activity to strengthen and improve the CETA program began well before the reauthorization act was passed, but has progressed slowly. The most notable undertakings have been the creation of the Office of the Inspector General, the initiation of two new comprehensive fraud and abuse prevention programs, a departmental review of the auditing system, an assessment of CETA technical assistance and training, and the creation of the Office of Management Assistance.

OFFICE OF THE INSPECTOR GENERAL (OIG)

Created under the Inspector Generals Act of 1978 as part of a government-wide reform, the Office of the Inspector General combined the former Office of Special Investigations and the departmental auditing staff. The OIG is located in the Office of the Secretary.

Fraud and Abuse Prevention Surveys (FAPS)

Early in fiscal year 1979, the OIG conducted the first two comprehensive reviews of CETA programs using a newly created Fraud and Abuse Prevention Survey. A FAPS review entails a month-long survey conducted on-site by a team that includes an auditor, an investigator, and a program analyst. Sponsors are required to respond to the report within 60 days of its issuance, and the OIG must follow up its review. No follow-up has yet been completed. The department had planned to conduct 6 reviews during FY 1979 and at least 20 more during 1980. After the first two reviews, however, it was decided that a major revision of the survey guide was necessary. After a three-month test of the survey instruments in Milwaukee, a condensed version of the survey guide is being developed.

The 20 reviews are currently expected to be carried out during 1980. It should be noted, however, that the FAPS program covers all departmental activities, not just CETA, and that other demands could affect the amount of investigatory activity that will be directed at CETA programs. Budgetary and staffing constraints may also limit its viability as a tool for program control.

The first two reviews were conducted during November and December of 1978 in the Mobile, Alabama, Consortium and the Cherokee Nation. They consisted of interviews with CETA staff members, local officials, and past and present CETA participants. In addition, contracts, payroll systems, participant files, and other accounting documents were reviewed.

The report on the Mobile Consortium (U.S. Department of Labor, 1979f) concentrated on management control systems for contracts, payroll, procurement, eligibility verification, and program planning. Conspicuously absent were any attempts to assess the effectiveness of the programs or the quality of the services provided. The Mobile CETA director characterized the report as generally helpful, although he noted that the investigators "were not all that knowledgeable about CETA" (*Employment and Training Reporter*, 1979, p. 195).

The focus of the Cherokee Nation report was on financial control systems, but it went much further than the Mobile Consortium review in assessing the services and effectiveness of the various CETA programs.

The report concluded that, "The lack of a well developed plan for determining the number and types of positions, specifying clearly attainable goals which would assure the transition from PSE employment into regular unsubsidized employment and the failure to implement monitoring procedures contributed to the general failure of the PSE program to meet regulatory requirements" (U.S. Department of Labor, 1979e, pp. 32-33).

Departmental Audits

Delays in auditing and the resolution of questioned costs have been chronic problems. In an attempt to coordinate the activities of the various auditing units scattered throughout the department, the OIG was given responsibility for this function. As yet, the new arrangement has not yet resulted in a significant improvement in either area, although the backlog of cases involving questioned costs has been reduced. Moreover, in spite of the rhetoric about increased emphasis in the detection of fraud and abuse in the CETA program, the number of prime sponsors that were audited was actually less in 1979 than in 1978 (Table 40).

Nonetheless, there are two promising developments. The first is the regulatory requirement for unified audits of CETA prime sponsors. Previously, prime sponsors audited their subrecipients and the DOL audited the prime sponsors; this practice resulted in duplication of effort. Furthermore, problems arose because the audits did not cover the same time periods. The unified audit system is intended to eliminate these problems by employing a single auditor to audit the entire prime sponsor operation; the cost of the audit will be shared by the sponsor and the department. However, like the FAPS program, the unified audit program appears to have been thwarted by funding problems. The OIG had planned to conduct 27 unified audits during FY 1979, but only one was conducted. That audit, in the "balance of Massachusetts," was funded entirely by the prime sponsor and was conducted only because the sponsor volunteered to participate.

In part, unified audits have not been conducted because there is no standard formula for dividing the costs between the sponsor and the OIG. The regulations provide only that the allocation be decided on an individual basis by "mutual agreement between the OIG and the recipient" (*Federal Register*, 1979a, p. 20031).

The second development in the area of departmental auditing was the creation of an intradepartmental review committee to assess auditing policies and recommend improvements. Although the committee report has not yet been released, the review revealed problems in the timely

TABLE 40   Department of Labor Office of Inspector General Audit
Activities, Fiscal 1978-1979

Programs to be Audited	Total Number of Units to be Audited	Numbers of Audits Required Annually	Actual Number of Audits/Reviews	
			FY 1978	FY 1979
CETA Titles I, II, and VI				
Prime Sponsor audits	460	230	169	125
CETA Title III				
Native American audits	174	174	157	165
CETA Title III				
Migrant Farm Labor audits	80	80	38	3
CETA Title IV				
Job Corps audits	120	120	31	11
CETA Subsponsor				
Report reviews	40,000	20,000	9,633	13,750

SOURCE: Semi-Annual Report of the Inspector General, U.S. Department of Labor,
June 1979, p. 6, and Semi-Annual Report of the Inspector General, April 1, 1979-
September 1979, p. 20.

development and distribution of audit guides to sponsors, as well as the
need for unified audits performed on a current basis.

Incident Reporting System

The Office of Investigation and Compliance (OIC) within the Employment
and Training Administration managed an investigatory program that was
later transferred to OIG. Under this program, the regional office was
required to send a Questionable Activity Report (QAR) to the OIC
whenever it became aware of a problem or potential problem within the
region. The national office of the ETA would then review the report and
assign responsibility for investigation to an appropriate agency—OIC
itself, the regional office, the prime sponsor, local law enforcement officials,
or in extreme cases, the FBI. The program was not particularly effective
for two reasons. First, there was little follow-up; cases were logged-in and
referrals made but the OIC seldom monitored the outcomes. Second, there
was no provision for anonymity within the system.

In the fall of 1979, the Office of the Inspector General instituted the

"Incident Reporting System" to replace the Questionable Activity Reports. Under this system, which covers all DOL programs, a report is sent directly to the OIG, which then decides what agency, if any, should investigate. This system guarantees anonymity to the individual filing the report.

OFFICE OF INVESTIGATION AND COMPLIANCE

Once the Office of the Inspector General was established and given responsibility for the Questionable Activities Reports, the activities of the Office of Investigation and Compliance (OIC) changed from reactive investigations to preventive monitoring reviews.

The OIC monitoring reviews bear some resemblance to the fraud and abuse prevention surveys conducted by the inspector general's staff. Like FAPS, they concentrate primarily on systems evaluations, but they focus less on financial questions. The surveys are conducted by a team of four to six individuals, one of whom generally has "an accounting background" and one of whom is an EEO specialist. The reports are based on two elements: interviews with participants, prime sponsor staff members, contractors, and local officials; and reviews of participant files, contracts, and other available reports and audits. Although the selection of sponsors to be reviewed is the responsibility of the OIC, the regional offices recommend the sponsors.

All of the 24 reviews planned for fiscal 1979 were completed, although follow-ups have not yet been performed. Fifty reviews are planned for 1980.

The most striking feature of the reports is their brevity. The booklet of interview questions is more than 90 pages and focuses on programmatic information. However, the reports do not reflect this information, but concentrate on shortcomings in financial accountability.

The OIC reviews and recommendations are directed to the regional office, not the prime sponsors. For example, one report, finding that the prime sponsor was monitoring subgrantees after contracts had been terminated, recommended that the regional office follow up to see that, in the future, monitoring would be accomplished while the program was in operation. Another report noted that the sponsor did not have a formal grievance procedure and recommended that the regional office provide technical assistance to the sponsor so that the procedure would be instituted as soon as possible.

The kind of monitoring done by OIC can be distinctive. But at this point, the roles of the OIC reviews and the FAPS are not clearly distinguished, and duplication of effort may result.

OFFICE OF MANAGEMENT ASSISTANCE

The Office of Management Assistance (OMA), mandated by the reauthorization act to provide management assistance to any prime sponsor seeking or needing such services, has been established within the Employment and Training Administration.

The office was set up in October 1979 after an extensive review of CETA technical assistance and training systems by a departmental task force. The report of the task force characterized the department's technical assistance and training efforts as "unorganized, uncoordinated, [and] crisis-oriented" (U.S. Department of Labor, 1979g, p. 5). The recommendations, numbering in the hundreds, covered such matters as long-range planning, prime sponsor participation in technical assistance policy, establishment of CETA field centers, and information distribution.

According to the task force report, the primary functions of OMA are to identify and coordinate the delivery of technical assistance and information. The report recommended that the OMA serve as a liaison between program officials in the national office, regional offices, the newly created OMA field centers, and other ETA units.

REGIONAL OFFICE ACTIVITIES

The federal representatives in each regional office are responsible for monitoring sponsor compliance with the law, the regulations, and the prime sponsors' plans. Formal assessments of prime sponsors' performance are conducted annually. In fiscal 1978, 50 of the 450 prime sponsors were assessed as having "serious problems"; the year before, 29 sponsors received this assessment. A serious problem rating indicates that major corrective action and/or technical assistance is required, and full funding is delayed until performance has improved. Of the 50 sponsors with serious problems, 41 received that rating for their PSE programs. The 1979 assessments found serious problems in 28 areas; PSE programs were the cause of the problems in 20 of these areas.

Federal representatives are expected to monitor prime sponsor programs on a continuing basis as well as on an annual basis. Very little change in regional monitoring has been noted since the reauthorization; a few sponsors thought it had actually diminished. Most of the sponsors in the survey characterized regional monitoring as primarily desk audit activity. One-third described it as an even combination of on-site and desk review.

In addition to their monitoring responsibilities, regional officials also provide technical assistance to prime sponsors and are the first line of contact between sponsors and the national offices. However, sponsors may be reluctant to seek aid from federal representatives who subsequently will assess their programs. The report of the Technical Assistance and Training Committee highlighted this problem (U.S. Department of Labor, 1979g, pp. 21-22):

In the last few years, a significant attitudinal change has been taking place between prime sponsors and the Regional Office. This has created almost an adversary relationship. There is an increasing tendency for prime sponsors to view regional staff as compliance enforcers rather than helpers. Prime sponsors are holding back on requesting technical assistance from the regions. They believe the staff is unable to provide it or are afraid the request will be looked upon as a deficiency in performance. The adversary relationship is thought to have been worsened by the new CETA legislation with its emphasis on prevention of fraud, mismanagement, and abuse.

SUMMARY

The impact of the independent monitoring units will probably be small. Prime sponsors, uncertain about DOL requirements concerning the organization and permissible activities of IMUs, have been slow to establish such units. Most of the units have been created from preexisting monitoring or evaluation units and do not represent a major change in organization or activities. Sponsors are generally reluctant to assess the IMUs at this point, but few expect that IMUs will result in better program operations or less fraud and abuse. Consequently, many sponsors view the IMU as an administrative burden that may create more problems than it solves.

Many sponsors have decided to use their IMUs to perform the eligibility verifications mandated by the reauthorization act. Although the verification requirements are clearly defined and quite extensive, most sponsors are going far beyond them in order to avoid the possibility of being held liable for ineligible participants. These procedures will reduce the number of ineligibles entering the program but will also require a significant investment of time and money. Some concern has been expressed that the procedures used to verify eligibility subject applicants to invasions of privacy and result in delays in enrollment.

Monitoring activity at the federal level has become increasingly self-initiated rather than reactive. Both the Office of Investigation and Compliance and the Office of the Inspector General have begun preventive review programs. However, only three reviews have been conducted by the inspector general, and neither office has done any follow-up; hence, the effects of the new programs cannot be assessed at this time.

7 Findings and Recommendations

The recommendations of the Committee on Evaluation of Employment and Training Programs are based on the committee's assessment of the effects of the 1978 CETA amendments on public service employment (PSE) programs. In developing its assessment, the committee focused its attention on the extent to which the new amendments are serving the objectives of the act. These objectives include increasing the proportion of jobs allotted to the most disadvantaged, preventing displacement of public employees by CETA workers, and providing temporary PSE jobs that lead to unsubsidized employment.

The committee has been sparing in its recommendations for major legislative changes because it is aware that repeated changes in policy, program direction, and funding levels have kept the CETA system in turmoil since its inception in 1973. The 1978 provisions were particularly traumatic.

The committee believes that CETA desperately needs a period of stability during which recent changes can be absorbed and results can be assessed. For this reason, the committee urges that major legislative changes in public service employment titles be deferred until CETA comes up for reauthorization in 1982, unless modifications are needed to counter

This chapter presents the recommendations of the Committee on Evaluation of Employment and Training Programs.

142

rising unemployment. However, the committee proposes some minor technical changes that would facilitate implementation of the 1978 amendments. The recommendations are presented in two major sections: program substance and program administration.

SUBSTANTIVE CHANGES IN PROGRAMS

The CETA reauthorization act made a number of substantive changes in the design of public service employment programs: it established a separate title (Title IID) to provide PSE jobs for the low-income, long-term unemployed; it lowered the authorized wages that could be paid to participants; and it required that training and other services be provided to enrollees to prepare them for unsubsidized jobs. This section deals with recommendations relating to eligibility criteria, selection of participants, wage provisions, and employability development activities.

ELIGIBILITY PROVISIONS AND PARTICIPANT SELECTION FOR PSE JOBS

One of the most persistent issues in CETA has been how to set eligibility criteria for public service jobs programs. Under the original act, the criteria were very broad; any person unemployed for 30 days was eligible. This loose screening requirement enabled PSE employers to select the most qualified participants from among the eligible applicants and adversely affected the enrollment of the most disadvantaged among the unemployed. Congress has repeatedly attempted to correct this situation, and the 1978 reauthorization act is the most recent effort in this direction. The following questions were addressed by the committee: (1) Are the revised eligibility criteria directing PSE jobs to the most disadvantaged? (2) What is the most effective way of assuring that the most needy applicants will be selected for jobs?

Findings

• Data from a sample of prime sponsor areas and other sources indicate that new enrollees are younger, poorer, less well educated, and more likely to be women and members of a minority group than those enrolled prior to the reauthorization act.

• Despite the requirement that special consideration be given to disabled and Vietnam-era veterans and to public assistance recipients, the percentage of disabled and Vietnam-era veterans is about the same as before the reauthorization. The proportion of AFDC recipients and other public welfare beneficiaries has risen but is still low compared with the share of AFDC participants in the eligible population.

• Because there are only minor differences in the eligibility criteria of Titles IID and VI, distinctions in PSE enrollees between the two titles are becoming less pronounced.

• To ensure that those most in need are selected from among the eligible population, the act has identified a number of groups to be given special consideration. Except for Vietnam-era veterans and welfare recipients, local sponsors are not mounting outreach efforts to recruit and select the specified target groups.

Recommendations

The committee endorses the objective of reserving PSE positions for those persons with the fewest alternative employment opportunities. The following recommendations are proposed to reinforce and enhance the act's effectiveness in meeting this goal.

Eligibility Requirements. The reauthorization act's eligibility requirements have effectively focused the PSE programs on the disadvantaged. Therefore, *the committee recommends that the eligibility criteria be retained.* However, should the scale of the Title VI program be increased significantly for countercyclical purposes, *the committee believes that the appropriateness of the Title VI criteria should be reexamined by the administration and by Congress.* It is uncertain at this time whether a significant number of the cyclically unemployed would qualify for Title VI jobs under the current eligibility requirements and whether under current time-consuming eligibility determination procedures, Title VI jobs could be filled rapidly enough to countercyclical pressures.

Groups Given Special Consideration. The multiplicity of target groups identified in the CETA legislation muddles the objectives of the act and undercuts the effectiveness of the targeting provisions of the act. *The committee recommends that Congress reduce the number of target groups or specify priorities among these groups.* It is recognized, however, that many groups will attempt to influence this decision of Congress. Limiting the number of federally designated target groups would not prevent local officials from identifying other groups in need of special assistance within their own jurisdictions.

Selection Procedures. The procedures used to choose PSE participants often do not result in the selection of those most in need of assistance. Reliance on "walk-in" applicants and the practice of referring the best-qualified applicants to openings tend to exclude persons who have the greatest difficulty in obtaining unsubsidized employment. This is particularly true for AFDC recipients. *The committee recommends that the Department of Labor direct prime sponsors to improve methods for recruiting severely disadvantaged applicants.* Closer control over intake processes and more objective methods of selection are among the methods proposed. To ensure that these applicants are referred to PSE jobs, *the committee recommends that prime sponsors establish objective rating systems for making referrals.* Under such systems, sponsors would assign numerical weights to characteristics such as educational attainment, family income, or welfare status and use these weights to rank applicants for referral to PSE openings.

To ascertain whether PSE employment offers participants an attractive alternative to welfare, *the committee recommends that the Department of Labor review the relative benefit levels provided by income transfer programs and CETA PSE positions.* Such a study should consider geographic variations in welfare benefit levels, variations due to family size, and the value of in-kind benefits such as food stamps and Medicaid in relation to PSE wages and fringe benefits. *The committee also recommends that the Department of Labor take additional steps to foster coordination and cooperation between the CETA and welfare systems.* The Department of Labor should review current policies on budget credits for placements to determine whether they act as a disincentive to interagency cooperation among the employment service, WIN, and CETA systems.

WAGES, JOBS, AND SERVICES

One of the most significant changes made by the CETA reauthorization act was the restriction on wages that could be paid to participants. The act lowered the national average PSE wage and provided for individual area adjustments above and below the average, based on the relationship between national average wages and the area's average wage for unsubsidized jobs. It also limited the extent to which local governments could supplement wages with their own funds. The intended effect of these provisions is to prevent CETA from attracting workers from private industry; discourage substitution of CETA workers for regular public employees; increase the number of unemployed persons that can be enrolled with available funds; and encourage the development of jobs that are appropriate for low-skilled disadvantaged workers.

Among the central questions addressed by the committee were: Can prime sponsors, in areas where prevailing wages are generally higher than allowable CETA average wages, establish suitable PSE jobs that meet both the new low-wage standards and the prevailing wage requirements? Will the low authorized wage result in "make-work" jobs rather than in employment that is useful to the community and beneficial to the participant?

Findings

The new CETA wage provisions are having a major impact on PSE wages and are affecting the types of jobs and services provided by PSE and the level of skills available among participants. Twenty-three of the 28 areas studied were required to reduce the average wage paid to new participants in 1979.

- The disparity between prevailing wages and permissible PSE wages is greater in some areas than in others because the calculation of average PSE wages for an area is largely based on private sector wages, but geographic variations in private sector wages do not necessarily correspond with variations in government wages.
- In most cases, sponsors adjusted to lower PSE wages by cutting back on professional, technical, paraprofessional, and craft positions and by establishing new positions at lower skill levels; many sponsors also planned to restructure positions. In a few cities, PSE programs were sharply curtailed because of the wage gap.
- In areas required to cut back wages, PSE activities are deemed to be less useful than they were in the past.
- Lower wages, along with restricted eligibility criteria, also appear to be affecting the skill level of participants. In three out of four areas new enrollees had fewer job qualifications than past participants.

It may be inferred that substitution will decrease as a result of the lower-wage provisions because the provisions have reduced the use of PSE for basic public service functions where substitution is likely to occur, lowered qualification of new enrollees, and increased the proportion of positions in nonprofit agencies.

Recommendations

Ideally, a CETA wage policy would maximize the participation of disadvantaged persons in PSE programs, while providing services that are useful to the community and beneficial for the participant. However, if a choice must be made between these goals, the entry of the disadvantaged into PSE jobs is closer to the central purpose of CETA.

Wage Policy. Because of their effectiveness in meeting the reauthorization objectives, the act's policies governing prevailing wage, average wage, maximum wage, and wage supplementation should be retained. However, some minor modifications in the wage provisions are suggested.

Area Adjustment of the National Average Wage. The national PSE average wage is adjusted for each area on the basis of the relationship between average wages for all public and private jobs in the area and the national average wage. The area adjustment factor is based largely on wages in private industry, which employs 82 percent of all workers. However, three-fourths of all PSE workers were employed in government agencies, and differences in private industry wages among areas are poor indicators of area differences in government wages. In areas where the PSE average wage is less than the wage prevailing for most entry level jobs in government, it is difficult to create PSE positions. Therefore *the Department of Labor should change the method for computing area wage adjustments. Consideration should be given to increasing the relative weight of government wages in this calculation.*

Supplementation Limits. Prior to the 1978 amendments, some sponsors, through supplements, established PSE positions that paid well above the average for unsubsidized jobs. These high-wage positions were also thought to be susceptible to substitution. To deter this practice, the reauthorization act forbids supplementation of Title IID wages and limits supplementation of Title VI wages to 10 percent of the maximum CETA wage in most areas and 20 percent in a few high-wage areas. *Because the limits on supplementation appear to be accomplishing their purposes, they should be retained for most areas. However, in cases where PSE wages, including supplements, are below the entry wages for almost all of the jobs in local government, Congress should authorize a 10 percent increase in supplements.*

Maximum Wage. There is no provision for adjusting the PSE maximum wage to reflect the effects of inflation. It remains fixed at $10,000 for about half of the CETA areas and may be as much as $12,000 for the remaining areas with above average wages. *To adjust for wage escalation, Congress should provide that the PSE maximum wage be modified annually by the procedure used for adjusting the PSE average wage.*

Further Review of Wage Effects. The impact of the new wage provisions should be reexamined by the Department of Labor and Congress in the fall of 1980 to provide an assessment of their long-term effects. By that time sponsors will have had more experience in dealing with the wage restrictions, and it will be possible to distinguish between problems that are intrinsic to the act and those that can be solved without legislative action.

TRANSITION AND EMPLOYABILITY DEVELOPMENT

The placement of enrollees in unsubsidized employment (transition) has been a constant, albeit sometimes neglected, goal of PSE programs. The reauthorization act reasserts this goal and prescibes employability development services to facilitate transition from PSE jobs to unsubsidized employment. PSE, particularly in Title IID, is to be more closely integrated with other training activities to enhance skills, provide useful work experience, and increase the prospects for regular employment.

The major issue examined by the committee was the extent to which congressional emphasis on transition is reflected in the employability development and placement activities of prime sponsors.

Findings

Job entry rates in a sample of study areas were slightly higher in fiscal 1979 than in fiscal 1978. The 18-month limit on duration of enrollment is a factor in this change. Most prime sponsors in the survey believed that the eligibility requirements under the reauthorization act would have the effect of increasing enrollments of those most difficult to place and would ultimately reduce the transition possibilities. Job entry rates for those terminating from the program may be affected by local employment prospects, as well as by the characteristics of participants, but the study emphasizes that management practices may also be a key factor. Despite slight increases in the job entry rate, widespread weaknesses in transition processes have been noted:

• Sponsors differ in the importance they attach to employability development plans (EDPs), the manner in which they prepare plans, and the extent to which they follow up on plans. Forty percent of the sponsors studied were not taking EDPs seriously, and nearly one-third did not have trained staff to carry out the function properly.

• More than one-third of the sponsors identified training and employability development as a problem in implementing new requirements. Many had not yet worked out strategies for integrating training with public service employment activities.

• Transition planning is inadequate in many jurisdictions, in part because sponsors lack job market information that is specific enough for planning placement activities.

Recommendations

Employability Development Plans. To make employability development plans meaningful *the Department of Labor should provide prime sponsors with EDP models and other technical assistance to aid them in developing staff capabilities in the area of transition.*

Job Development Information Needs. The Department of Labor should prepare and disseminate examples of techniques and procedures for identifying, soliciting, and developing job opportunities for CETA terminees. These should be based on the experience with the job bank and with other automated information systems in the employment service, the unemployment insurance system, and the CETA system.

Further Research. Two major obstacles hindered the committee's attempt to assess the effects of the reauthorization act and the variations in local management policies on job entry rates. First, the effects of the act were not reflected by most of the terminations at the time of the survey, because the individuals affected had entered the program before the new provisions of the reauthorization act were implemented. Second, there were wide variations in the reporting procedures used by prime sponsors, and these variations precluded an accurate assessment of placement results. The committee believes that at least one year of experience with termination under the reauthorization act is essential for an accurate assessment of its impact. *The committee, therefore, recommends that the Department of Labor arrange for supplementary surveys to be conducted when sufficient time has elasped to identify and measure the effects of the 1978 amendments on transition and the relationship between placement results and local management policies and practices.*

PROGRAM ADMINISTRATION

The CETA reauthorization act sought to tighten program accountability throughout the system and attempted to simplify administration by reducing the amount of paperwork involved in the grant application process. The findings and recommendations in this section of the chapter focus on the implementation of legislative and other programmatic changes and their effects on the management of CETA programs.

Monitoring and Eligibility Verification

The reauthorization act and accompanying regulations mandated specific actions to reduce the incidence of fraud and abuse and to tighten controls and accountability. Independent monitoring units (IMUs) were to be established at the prime sponsor and subcontractor levels to monitor all program activities and management practices. At the federal level, responsibility for compliance was centered in a newly created Office of the Inspector General. The act also required prime sponsors to establish an acceptable system for eligibility determination and verification and defined the liability of prime sponsors.

The central question is whether the Department of Labor and prime sponsors are implementing effectively the monitoring and eligibility verification provisions of the act and whether the oversight activity adversely affects other program activities.

Findings

Most sponsors in the study sample did some monitoring before the reauthorization act. However, the creation of IMUs has given prominence and more structure to this activity. At the time of the survey, some sponsors had not yet set up IMUs and few had arranged for monitoring units at the subcontractor level. The establishment of IMUs was hampered by uncertainties relating to the scope of IMU activities and the degree of IMU independence. In areas that had established IMUs, the size and quality of staff posed problems.

• Nearly all IMUs report to CETA administrators who define their investigative and management review functions and determine procedures for corrective action. Under these circumstances, the degree of independence is likely to vary considerably.

• The range of subjects covered by IMUs reflects a lack of direction. Over three-fourths of the sponsors in the study sample expect to increase attention to questions of eligibility and wages, but maintenance of effort investigations are not being pressed.

• In some instances, IMU staff were reported to lack specialized skills needed for effective monitoring.

One of the consequences of assigning liability for ineligible participants to prime sponsors is that sponsors have become reluctant to delegate responsibility for eligibility verification to the employment service or other organizations. Procedures for determining and documenting eligibility are detailed and time consuming. Sponsors report that the processing of new enrollees is slowed as a result. In the event of a cyclical rise in unemployment, these procedures might prevent sufficient increases in enrollment.

At the national level, responsibility for program monitoring of CETA is assigned to a newly created Office of the Inspector General, various auditing units, and an Office of Investigation and Compliance. Problems of coordination, policy differences, and inadequate funding have hampered the activities of those offices. For the most part, federal monitoring is performed by regional representatives of the Employment and Training Administration. Many of these regional representatives handle technical assistance as well as compliance, and this dual responsibility hampers their effectiveness in both roles.

Recommendations

Monitoring. The quality of the staff of independent monitoring units varies considerably. Many IMUs lack personnel with accounting and investigatory skills. *The Department of Labor should provide training and technical assistance to IMUs and to regional monitoring personnel.*

Sponsors are uncertain about what constitutes fraud and abuse and which cases should be referred to federal investigatory personnel. *The Department of Labor should develop a monitoring guide for sponsors and publish examples of effective sponsor monitoring systems. The department should also distribute information about problems which have been discovered and the issues involved in their resolution.*

Federal representatives are currently in the untenable position of monitoring programs for which they have provided technical assistance. Prime sponsors, for their part, are reluctant to ask for help from regional staff who will subsequently monitor their programs. *The committee recommends that technical assistance and monitoring functions be separated at the regional level.*

Coordination of Monitoring Activities. Monitoring occurs at all administrative levels. At the national level, both the inspector general and the Office of Investigation and Compliance in the Employment and Training Administration have begun surveys to prevent fraud and abuse; regional offices prepare evaluations through annual performance assessments; and prime sponsors have established monitoring units that perform day-to-day reviews. Very often, however, the relationship among these organizations is unclear, leading to duplication of effort. *The Department of Labor should review the monitoring activites of all levels of administration in the CETA system to clarify the role of each and to integrate monitoring efforts.*

The DOL unified audit system (a plan for auditing subcontractors and prime sponsors simultaneously) has not been implemented, in part because no rules have been developed for distributing audit expenses between sponsors and the Office of the Inspector General. *Regulations for allocating the cost of unified audits should be developed by the Department of Labor, and steps should be taken to implement unified auditing.*

Eligibility Verification and Liability. Because of a stricter interpretation of liability, and uncertainty as to how liability provisions will be enforced, prime sponsors have developed elaborate systems for eligibility verification. These procedures are slowing down enrollment and causing some applicants to drop out of the system. *The Department of Labor should clarify its liability policy and begin to enforce the liability provisions of the act. Liability policies should be consistent across regions.* Among the items that should be explicitly stated are the dollar amount at which misspent monies are considered "too great," what constitutes an "effective system" of eligibility verification, and the circumstances under which prime sponsors must notify national or regional officials if ineligible participants are discovered.

Present procedures for eligibility verification are excessively complex in some areas, and may not be justified by the incidence of ineligibles entering the PSE program. To relate the costs of eligibility determinations more realistically to the incidence of ineligibility, *the Department of Labor should develop a flexible procedure, permitting less frequent sample verifications in areas where improper enrollments are uncommon.*

THE PLANNING SYSTEM

The objectives of the CETA planning system are (1) to formulate goals on the basis of local needs; (2) to involve the community in the planning process; and (3) to provide a systematic basis for federal evaluation of budgets and operations. As CETA evolved, the third objective overshadowed the first two; plans became an awesome collection of grant applications for specific titles. The CETA reauthorization act sought to simplify planning documents and reduce paperwork. The act also required that planning councils become more representative of the community. The issue is whether these planning objectives are being met.

Findings

• The study finds that the planning documents must contain more detail under the reauthorization act than in the past. Most sponsors consider the present plans more time-consuming, no easier, and no more useful than previous plans.

• In many cases, demographic and labor market data are among the items not available in a form that is useable for planning.

• Annual plans are still a series of grant applications rather than an integrated and comprehensive area plan. The basic problem stems from the ambiguity of the legislation. On the one hand CETA provides local authorities with flexibility to allocate funds on the basis of local needs, and on the other hand, it requires local sponsors to comply with nationally determined objectives and priorities.

• Most of the sponsors in the study sample were expanding the membership of advisory councils, but the influence of planning councils does not appear to have grown; the decision-making process has remained largely centralized in the CETA administrator's office.

• At the time of the study, prime sponsors were beginning to activate Private Industry Councils (PICs) to increase private sector participation in CETA. The study finds that the relationship between PICs and advisory councils is still evolving. There appears to be some potential for duplication and fragmentation of operations as well as planning.

Recommendations

Improving the Quality of Plans. To serve as a blueprint for action, plans should describe the local labor market setting and identify the population in need of service and the institutions that can provide those services. Evaluation of the effectiveness of various approaches that have been tried in prior years should be an integral part of the planning documents. Information on other federal, state, and local programs in the community—economic development, community development, housing, energy conservation, and health—should also be incorporated in local plans. It is essential that plans contain information that is useful for management at various levels of government. *The committee recommends that the Department of Labor provide greater assistance to sponsors for improving the quality of plans so that they may serve as a better basis for comprehensive planning.* This can be done through training sessions and materials on the principles and methodology of planning. In prime sponsor jurisdictions that are too large for central planning, technical assistance should also be provided to program agents and other subjurisdictions.

Labor Market Information. One of the pervasive problems in planning is the lack of appropriate information on the labor force, employment outlook by industry and occupation, and unemployment in the population as a whole and among particular groups such as women, minorities, and youth. The major source of this information is the state employment security agency. Because labor market information is prepared for many different users, the data provided to CETA sponsors are often outdated, incompatible with the geographic unit covered by the prime sponsor, or not sufficiently detailed for the specific needs of CETA users. *The committee recommends that the Department of Labor devote more attention, staff, and resources to labor market information systems appropriate for CETA planning.* Information systems should be improved in several ways: research should be undertaken on the kinds of information needed for analytical and operating purposes; data sources should be examined and data-gathering systems coordinated; and techniques for estimating unemployment, occupational demand, and the supply of trained workers should be improved. The system needs quality controls and methods for disseminating information to users on a timely basis. It is especially important to involve CETA prime sponsors, employment security agencies, and education agencies in joint efforts to produce labor market information that is more relevant for local use.

Reduction in Paperwork. Although the reauthorization act attempted to reduce paperwork, the study found that the master and annual plan requirements are no less onerous than past requirements. *The committee recommends that the Department of Labor, in consultation with prime sponsors, establish a task force to review the guidelines and eliminate requirements for nonessential details.* Statistical profiles of the eligible population for each separate program, occupational summaries of public service jobs, and planning budgets are among the items identified by respondents as excessively detailed.

Stabilizing Appropriations and Allocations. Congressional delays in appropriations and uncertainties in funding levels have frustrated planning and administration. *The committee recommends that the administration and Congress use the authority available under the act for advance funding of CETA except for Title VI.* This would permit more orderly planning and management of programs and allow more time for refining and relaying instructions, and for providing technical assistance and training for CETA staff. The exception has been made for countercyclical PSE programs under Title VI because the level of Title VI appropriations is tied to changes in unemployment rates.

ADMINISTRATION AND INSTITUTIONAL RELATIONS

The CETA reauthorization act has added to the accumulation of prescriptions and proscriptions that have made public service employment programs increasingly difficult to manage. It is questionable whether prime sponsors have sufficient resources and staff to carry out their responsibilities under the 1978 amendments or to handle an increase in enrollees that would accompany an expansion of PSE or a welfare reform program.

The reauthorization act failed to resolve the long-standing problem of the federal-local relations in the administration of CETA. The original act was deliberately ambivalent in delineating roles. In an effort to compromise differing views, it shifted the administration of manpower programs to state and local officials but mandated a substantial oversight role for the federal establishment. This set the stage for continuing tensions. In some respects these have been exacerbated by the reauthorization amendments that inherently give greater weight to the federal role, at least in the introductory phases. The issue is how best to reconcile the respective roles and interests of federal and local officials.

Also unresolved by the reauthorization act are relationships between CETA prime sponsors and state employment security agencies. In effect, CETA established a network of offices, some of whose functions overlap those of the employment service system. Congress did not, in the reauthorization act, attempt to clarify the relationship. The committee is concerned with how best to utilize the special competence of both systems to promote the objectives of manpower programs.

Findings

• During the transition year, administration of public service employment programs was seriously affected by delays in funding, shifts in the level of allocations, and changes in enrollment goals. Moreover, the introduction of new regulations and changes in policies kept operations in constant turmoil.

• Looking beyond the first year, sponsors in the study sample believed that complying with wage provisions, tracking the length of stay of enrollees, providing employability development and training, and determining and verifying eligibility would pose long-term operating problems.

• Programmatic changes in PSE, along with requirements for monitoring, planning, and reporting have increased record keeping and other administrative activities. The staff and resource implications of these changes are considerable. Although their full costs were not realized at the time of the survey, administrative cost ratios did increase. Furthermore, staff turnover and morale reflected the strains and burdens associated with the growth and instability of the system.

• The reauthorization act, by increasing specifications for eligibility, wages, tenure, and other program requirements, has tended to reduce local flexibility.

• Greater interaction between local sponsors and federal officials produced frictions that centered around interpretation of rules, pressures for meeting enrollment goals, and implementation of new provisions.

• The close working relationships between the employment service and prime sponsors, fostered by the 1976 amendments to CETA and the expansion of public service jobs programs in 1977-1978, have begun to erode. Although the use of employment service offices for placement of enrollees has increased in some areas, there is less dependence on the employment service for eligibility determination and verification.

Recommendations

Staffing. The committee recommends that the Department of Labor study the staffing and cost implications of implementing amendments to CETA. Unless sufficient resources are made available, some of the act's provisions, such as monitoring or preparing employability development plans, may become pro forma exercises. *The committee also recommends that the DOL Office of Management Assistance provide technical assistance to local sponsors to improve merit systems, personnel standards, staff development practices, and organizational structures* and to take other steps to improve employee morale and reduce turnover.

Federal-Local Relations. The tensions arising from the grasp of the "feds" and the reach of the "locals" may be inevitable in a decentralized block grant program. However, it may be possible to reduce some of these tensions. Most of the friction during the transition year stemmed from the delays and lack of uniformity in the interpretation of the regulations. *To minimize this problem, the committee recommends that Congress allow more time for the implementation of new legislation. The Department of Labor, in turn, should allow more time for dissemination and review of proposed rules.* A longer lead time would permit more time for planning and training of local staff, and would reduce misunderstandings.

Employment Service–CETA Relations. The committee recommends that the Department of Labor arrange for a study of incentives that affect coordination in intake and job placement services to determine whether changes in placement credits or other measures would induce closer coordination.

A more basic problem, however, is the coexistence of two national networks with related functions. The reauthorization act required that the secretary of labor recommend improvements in the Wagner-Peyser Act to ensure coordination with CETA, but the Department of Labor has not yet filed its report. *The committee recommends that Congress establish an independent commission to examine the roles and functions of both CETA and the employment service and to propose methods for harmonizing the two manpower systems.*

Coordination with Other Agencies. Emphasis on basic education and skill training for youth in the administration's 1981 budget proposals would necessitate coordination between CETA and vocational education agencies. The administration's welfare reform proposals would depend on close coordination between CETA and welfare agencies. *The committee sees a need for the Department of Labor to study the coordination of CETA agencies with the education and welfare systems, and with Private Industry Councils (PICs).*

References

Congressional Record (1978a) 124(124):H8164.

Congressional Record (1978b) 124(133):S13953, S13955, S13968

Employment and Training Reporter (1978) 10(4):51-2. "50 Sponsors Earn 'Serious Problem' Rating in FY '78, up from 29 in '77." (Washington, D.C.: Manpower Information, Inc.)

Employment and Training Reporter (1979) 11(8):195. "FAPs Program is Far Behind Schedule; Inspector General is Reassessing It." (Washington, D.C.: Manpower Information, Inc.)

Federal Register (1979a) Vol. 44, no. 65 (April 3), Rules and Regulations. "Part IX, Department of Labor, Employment and Training Administration; CETA Regulations; Final Rule."

Federal Register (1979b) Vol. 44, no. 156 (August 10), Rules and Regulations. "Part V, Department of Labor, Employment and Training Administration; Public Service Employment; Procedures for Waivers of Time Limitations."

Institute for Manpower Program Analysis, Consultation and Training, Inc. (1978) *Evaluation of CETA/SESA Linkage Demonstration Projects.* Prepared by Frederick Manzara and Associates. Final Report. U.S. Department of Labor Report MEL 78-11; Contract No. 23-27-77-01. Minneapolis, Minn.

National Association of Counties (1979) CETA Information Update, July 13, 1979. Available from National Association of Counties, 1735 New York Avenue, N.W., Washington, D.C.

National Commission for Employment (formerly Manpower) Policy (1978) "Summary of Findings and Recommendations." Volume 1 in *Job Creation Through Public Service Employment.* Washington, D.C.

National Commission for Employment (formerly Manpower) Policy (1979) *Monitoring the Public Service Employment Program: The Second Round.*

Prepared by The Brookings Institution under the direction of Dr. Richard Nathan. Special Report No. 32. Washington, D.C.

National Council on Employment Policy (1978) *The Case for CETA Reauthorization: Continued Decentralization and Decategorization.* A Statement by the National Council on Employment Policy. Washington, D.C.

National Council on Employment Policy (1979) *Wagner-Peyser: Time for a Change?* A Policy Statement by the National Council on Employment Policy. Washington, D.C.

National Planning Association (1977) *The National Manpower Survey of the Criminal Justice System.* Volume I, Summary Report. Washington, D.C.: U.S. Government Printing Office.

National Research Council (1978) *CETA: Manpower Programs Under Local Control.* Prepared by W. Mirengoff and L. Rindler. Committee on Evaluation of Employment and Training Programs. Washington, D.C.: National Academy of Sciences.

National Research Council (1980) *CETA: Assessment of Public Service Employment Programs.* Prepared by W. Mirengoff, L. Rindler, H. Greenspan, and S. Seablom. Committee on Evaluation of Employment and Training Programs. Washington, D.C.: National Academy of Sciences.

Ohio State University (1978) *CETA Prime Sponsor Management Decisions and Program Goal Achievement.* Prepared by Randall B. Ripley and Associates. U.S. Department of Labor R&D Monograph 56. Washington, D.C.: U.S. Government Printing Office.

Ohio State University (1979) *Areawide Planning in CETA.* Prepared by Randall B. Ripley and Associates. U.S. Department of Labor R&D Monograph 74. Washington, D.C.: U.S. Government Printing Office.

Ohio State University Research Foundation (1979a) *A Formative Evaluation of the Private Sector Initiative Program.* Report No. 1. Prepared by Randall B. Ripley and Associates, Mershon Center. U.S. Department of Labor Report MEL 79-14; Contract No. 24-39-79-01. Columbus, Ohio.

Ohio State University Research Foundation (1979b) *A Formative Evaluation of the Private Sector Initiative Program.* Report No. 2. Prepared by Randall B. Ripley and Associates, Mershon Center. Available from NTIS (PB80-113079), Springfield, Va.

U.S. Congress (1973) *Comprehensive Employment and Training Act of 1973.* Public Law 93-230. 93rd Congress. Washington, D.C.: U.S. Government Printing Office.

U.S. Congress (1974) *Emergency Jobs and Unemployment Assistance Act of 1974.* Public Law 93-567. 93rd Congress. Washington, D.C.: U.S. Government Printing Office.

U.S. Congress (1976a) *Emergency Employment Project Amendments of 1976.* House Committee on Education and Labor, H.R. 94-804. 94th Congress, 2nd Session. Washington, D.C.: U.S. Government Printing Office.

U.S. Congress (1976b) *Emergency Jobs Programs Extension Act of 1976.* Senate Committee on Labor and Public Welfare, S.R. 94-883. 94th Congress, 2nd Session. Washington, D.C.: U.S. Government Printing Office.

U.S. Congress (1976c) *Emergency Jobs Programs Extension Act of 1976.* Committee of Conference, H.R. 94-1514. 94th Congress, 2nd Session. Washington, D.C.: U.S. Government Printing Office.

U.S. Congress (1976d) *Emergency Jobs Programs Extension Act of 1976.* Public Law 94-444. 94th Congress. Washington, D.C.: U.S. Government Printing Office.

U.S. Congress (1978a) *Comprehensive Employment and Training Act Amendments of 1978.* House Committee on Education and Labor, H.R. 95-1124. 95th Congress, 2nd Session. Washington, D.C.: U.S. Government Printing Office.

U.S. Congress (1978b) *Comprehensive Employment and Training Act Amendments of 1978.* Committee on Human Resources, S.R. 95-891. 95th Congress, 2nd Session. Washington, D.C.: U.S. Government Printing Office.

U.S. Congress (1978c) *Comprehensive Employment and Training Act Amendments of 1978.* Committee of Conference, S.R. 95-1325. 95th Congress, 2nd Session. Washington, D.C.: U.S. Government Printing Office.

U.S. Congress (1978d) *Comprehensive Employment and Training Act Amendments of 1978.* Public Law 95-524. 95th Congress. Washington, D.C.: U.S. Government Printing Office.

U.S. Congress (1979a) *Department of Labor's Administration of the Comprehensive Employment and Training Act.* House Committee on Government Operations, H.R. 96-657. 96th Congress, 1st Session. Washington, D.C.: U.S. Government Printing Office.

U.S. Congress (1979b) *Labor, HEW Appropriations Bill, Fiscal Year 1980.* House Appropriations Committee, H.R. 96-244. 96th Congress, 1st Session. Washington, D.C.: U.S. Government Printing Office.

U.S. Department of Labor (n.d.) CETA Monitoring Reports (unpublished). Office of the Inspector General, Office of Investigation and Compliance. Reports for: Arlington County, Virginia; Burlington County, New Jersey; Colorado Springs, Colorado; Fairfax, Virginia Consortium; Hillsboro County, New Hampshire; Lincoln City, Nebraska; Middle Georgia Consortium (Macon); Providence, Rhode Island.

U.S. Department of Labor (1977) "Factors Associated with AFDC Participation in CETA Title VI." Unpublished report. Employment and Training Administration. Work Incentive Program (WIN).

U.S. Department of Labor (1979a) *The Comprehensive Employment and Training Act Amendments of 1978—Forms Preparation Handbook.* Employment and Training Administration. ET Handbook No. 311.

U.S. Department of Labor (1979b) *Employment and Earnings* 26(5):139-141.

U.S. Department of Labor (1979c) *Employment and Training Evaluation Report—1979.* Prepared by the Employment and Training Administration and the Office of the Assistant Secretary for Policy, Evaluation, and Research.

U.S. Department of Labor and U.S. Department of Health, Education, and Welfare (1979d) *Employment and Training Report of the President.* Washington, D.C.: U.S. Government Printing Office.

U.S. Department of Labor (1979e) "Fraud and Abuse Prevention Survey Report. Cherokee Nation—Tahlequah, Oklahoma (November 27, 1979–December 20, 1978)." Office of the Inspector General. Unpublished report.

U.S. Department of Labor (1979f) "Fraud and Abuse Prevention Survey Report. Mobile Consortium—Mobile, Alabama (November 20, 1978–December 22, 1978)." Office of the Inspector General. Unpublished report.

U.S. Department of Labor (1979g) *Review of the Employment and Training Administration's Technical Assistance and Training System.* Prepared by the Employment and Training Administration. Washington, D.C.: U.S. Government Printing Office.

U.S. Department of Labor (1979h) *Semi-Annual Report of the Inspector General.* October 1, 1978–March 31, 1979. Office of the Inspector General.

U.S. Department of Labor (1979i) *Semi-Annual Report of the Inspector General.* April 1, 1979–September 30, 1979. Office of the Inspector General.

U.S. Department of Labor (1980) *Wage Differences Among Large City Governments and Comparisons with Industry and Federal Pay, 1977-1979.* Bureau of Labor Statistics. Report 596.

U.S. General Accounting Office (1978) *Information on the Buildup in Public Service Jobs.* Report by the Comptroller General of the United States. HRD-78-57. Washington, D.C.

U.S. General Accounting Office (1979) *Moving Participants From Public Service Employment Programs Into Unsubsidized Jobs Needs More Attention.* Report by the Comptroller General of the United States. HRD-79-101. Washington, D.C.

University of Texas at Austin (1978) *The Transition From Public Service Employment to Unsubsidized Jobs in the Private and Public Sectors.* Final Report. Prepared by Policy Research Project of the Lyndon B. Johnson School of Public Affairs. U.S. Department of Labor Report MEL 78-14; Contract No. 24-48-78-01. Austin, Tex.

Westat, Inc. (1977) "Methodology." Technical Report No. 1 in *Continuous Longitudinal Manpower Survey.*

Westat, Inc. (1979) "Postprogram Experiences and Pre/Post Comparisons for Terminees Who Entered CETA during Fiscal Year 1976 (July 1975–June 1976)." Follow-up Report No. 2 (18 months after entry) in *Continuous Longitudinal Manpower Survey.* Available from NTIS (PB-310 119/4ST), Springfield, Va.

APPENDIXES

Appendix A:
Statistical Tables

TABLE A-1 CETA Appropriations, by Title, Fiscal 1974-1981 (millions of dollars)

Title[a]	Fiscal 1974[b]	Fiscal 1975	Fiscal 1976		Fiscal 1977	Fiscal 1978	Fiscal 1979	Fiscal 1980	Budget Fiscal 1981
			July 1975-June 1976	July-Sept. 1976					
TOTAL	2,265.6	3,742.8	5,741.8	597.6	8,052.8	8,124.9	10,289.7	8,127.6	10,305.4
Comprehensive Manpower Programs	1,190.0	1,819.4	1,848.4	453.8	3,480.7	2,267.9	2,360.7	2,915.0	2,917.9
I (II A, B, C)	1,010.0	1,580.0	1,580.0	395.4	1,880.0	1,880.0	1,914.1	2,054.0	2,117.0
III	180.0	239.4	268.4	58.4	1,600.7[c]	387.9	371.6	536.0	650.9
VII[d]	—	—	—	—	—	—	75.0	325.0	150.0
Youth Programs	455.6	648.4	668.4	43.8	869.1	1,173.0	2,023.6	2,100.6	2,789.4
IV	150.0	175.0	140.0	43.8	274.1	417.0	1,238.4[e]	1,492.0	1,950.4[h]
Summer youth	305.6	473.4	528.4	—	595.0	756.0	785.2	608.6	839.0

Public Service Employment Programs	620.0	1,275.0	3,225.0	100.0	3,703.0	4,684.0	5,905.3	3,112.0	4,598.0
II (II D)	370.0	400.0	1,600.0[f]	100.0	524.0	1,016.0[g]	2,500.9	1,485.0	2,554.0
VI	250.0	875.0	1,625.0	—	3,179.0	3,668.0[g]	3,404.4	1,627.0	2,044.0

SOURCE: Employment and Training Administration, U.S. Department of Labor.

[a]Beginning in fiscal 1979, titles redesignated as shown in parentheses.

[b]Appropriations for Department of Labor manpower programs corresponding with Titles I and II of CETA, and for the Emergency Employment Act corresponding with Title VI.

[c]Includes $233.3 million for Young Adult Conservation Corps, also funds for veterans programs (HIRE), skill training improvement (STIP), and other youth programs.

[d]Private sector initiatives, beginning in fiscal 1979.

[e]Beginning in fiscal 1979, includes funds for youth employability development projects and for the Young Adult Conservation Corps.

[f]$1,200 million authorized under Title II for both Titles II and VI.

[g]Forward funded from 1977 appropriation under the Economic Stimulus Appropriations Act.

[h]Includes $1,125 million for new youth legislation, proposed for later transmittal.

NOTE: Details may not add to totals due to rounding.

TABLE A-2 Selected Characteristics of Title II (IID) and Title VI Participants, Fiscal 1975-1979 (percentage distribution)

Selected Characteristics	Fiscal 1975	Fiscal 1976[a]	Fiscal 1977	Fiscal 1978	Fiscal 1979			
					Oct.-Dec.	Oct.-March	April-June[b]	April-September[b]
NUMBER SERVED	298,556	747,158	928,239	1,218,722	660,257	892,943	801,024	955,200
Sex: Male	68	65	63	61	57	56	55	55
Female	32	35	37	39	43	44	45	45
Age: 21 and under	23	22	20	21	20	19	21	22
22-44	64	64	65	65	65	65	64	63
45-54	9	9	9	8	10	9	9	9
55 and over	5	5	6	5	6	6	6	6
Race/Ethnic group:[c]								
White	69	66	69	67	(69)[d]	(66)[d]	(67)[d]	(67)[d]
White (nonhispanic)	NA	NA	NA	NA	58	57	55	55
Black	22	24	25	28	(28)[d]	(29)[d]	(28)[d]	(30)[d]
Black (nonhispanic)	NA	NA	NA	NA	28	29	28	30
Hispanic	(7)[e]	(11)[e]	(NA)[e]	(10)[e]	11	9	12	13
Other	9	10	6	5	4	5	5	3
Education: 0-11 years	26	26	25	26	25	26	28	28
12 years	44	43	42	41	44	43	44	43
13 years and over	30	32	32	33	30	30	28	29
Economic Status:								
AFDC recipient	6	6	9	11	11	11	12	12
Public assistance, other	8	8	8	8	6	7	7	8

	44	45	60	78	77	80	83	85
Economically disadvantaged[f]								
Family income below poverty level[g]	44	45	60	NA	58	63	63	65
Handicapped:	3	3	4	4	4	4	4	5
Veterans: Total[h]	NA	NA	24	23	19	19	17	17
Special[h]	NA	9	7	5	4	4	3	3
Disabled	NA	0	1	1	1	1	1	1
Unemployment Insurance Claimant:	13	14	16	14	14	13	12	11

SOURCE: Quarterly Summary of Participant Characteristics, Employment and Training Administration, U.S. Department of Labor.

[a]July 1, 1975 to June 30, 1976.

[b]Characteristics shown are for individuals served in the third and fourth quarters of fiscal 1979. However, prime sponsors that did not rewrite their Title II and VI grants on March 31, 1979 may have reported cumulative totals for the first three quarters of fiscal 1979. No adjustment has been made to exclude cumulative reports.

[c]Participants for whom racial characteristics were not available were excluded from the number served in calculating the racial characteristic percentages.

[d]Due to changes in reporting categories, race/ethnic group data reported for 1979 are not comparable with earlier years. Assuming that hispanics were classified as white in previous years, the numbers in parentheses would be comparable with those shown for fiscal 1975-1978.

[e]Included in figures for other race/ethnic groups.

[f]Definition was expanded in fiscal 1978 to include persons with family income between the poverty level set by the Office of Management and Budget and 70 percent of the lower living income standard set by the Bureau of Labor Statistics. In fiscal 1979, the definition was expanded to include members of certain institutionalized populations.

[g]Proportion of participants with family income below the poverty level set by the Office of Management and Budget.

[h]Veterans who served in Indochina or Korea between 1964 and 1975.

NOTE: Details may not add to 100 percent due to rounding.

169

TABLE A-3   Public Service Employment Authorized Average Wage and Lowest Wage for Municipal Government Employees in Selected Occupations

Region and City	Date of BLS Survey	PSE Average Wage FY 1979	Lowest City Wage for:			
			Typists Class B	Refuse Collectors	Laborers	Janitors, Porters, and Cleaners
Northeast						
Boston	10/78	$7,805	$7,280	$ – [a]	$ 8,528	$ 8,216
New York	5/79	8,690	7,020	14,976	13,312	7,904
Philadelphia	9/78	7,855	9,880	10,816	10,816	9,984
Pittsburgh	2/79	8,129	9,360	15,600	11,232	7,072
North Central						
Chicago	6/79	8,417	6,760	16,224	12,064	11,232
Indianapolis	9/79	7,920	7,020	9,226	9,152	9,464
Detroit	1/79	9,662	9,880	13,728	13,728	10,608
Kansas City, Mo.	9/79	7,553	6,240	8,320	6,968	7,280
St. Louis	8/78	8,050	7,280	8,944	8,528	6,968
Cleveland	8/79	8,352	7,020	11,232	10,400	8,528
Columbus	4/79	7,351	9,360	12,896	9,568	10,816
Milwaukee	7/79	7,754	8,840	12,064	11,856	10,192
South						
Washington, D.C.	10/78	9,540	7,280	11,856	9,152	9,776
Jacksonville	12/78	6,667	6,500	6,656	6,448	6,448
Atlanta	5/79	7,898	8,329	7,488	7,696	6,656
New Orleans	9/79	7,121	6,760	– [a]	7,280	– [a]
Memphis	11/78	6,833	5,720	8,017	6,452	6,061
Dallas	4/79	7,596	7,280	7,904	7,280	6,864
Houston	9/78	8,338	6,240	10,816	7,696	6,240
San Antonio	2/79	6,635	5,980	8,235	6,448	5,824
West						
Phoenix	7/78	6,941	7,280	9,360	8,736	8,736
Los Angeles	10/78	7,913	8,320	10,816	9,984	7,904
San Diego	11/78	6,962	7,280	11,648	8,944	8,528
San Francisco	3/79	8,935	8,320	– [a]	12,480	9,984
Denver	3/79	7,812	6,240	12,480	11,440	8,736
Seattle	1/79	8,251	9,100	– [a]	12,480	10,400

SOURCE: PSE average wage data from Employment and Training Administration; city wage data from Municipal Government Wage Surveys for 1978 and 1979, Bureau of Labor Statistics, U.S. Department of Labor.

[a] Not municipal positions in these cities.

Appendix B:
Methodology Statements

DESCRIPTION OF SAMPLE AND STUDY METHODOLOGY

Although data for the committee's report were drawn from a number of sources, the primary source was the field observations in a stratified random sample of 28 prime sponsors drawn from a universe of 383.[1] To select the sample, the universe was first stratified by 4 types of sponsors (city, county, consortium, and balance of state), by 2 classes of population level (above and below one million), and by 2 classes based on the rate of unemployment (above and below 6.5 percent). The 16 strata were combined into 11 cells, and the prime sponsors were selected within each cell by a random procedure.

As in prior surveys, information from the committee's report was obtained by resident field research associates (FRAs), most of whom are faculty members at universities who have been engaged in manpower research. FRAs used structured, standardized guides to interview local CETA administrators, elected officials, chairmen of advisory committees, employment service officials, community-based organization officials, union representatives, and others familiar with the area's manpower problems and the administration of CETA programs. The total interview time in each area was about one week. Moreover, most FRAs had been monitoring the CETA program in their areas for several years and had developed considerable knowledge of the program. The committee relies on summary observations and judgments of field research associates as well as on the survey data.

Interview data are supplemented by statistics from prime sponsor records as well as from reports of the Employment and Training Administration of the U.S. Department of Labor and from other sources.

The FRAs' interviews were conducted in June and July 1979, only a few months after the provisions of the CETA reauthorization act became fully effective. Due to the magnitude of the changes dictated by the act, the Employment and Training Administration, which sponsored the project, was anxious to obtain an early reading of the effect of its implementation. Officials of the Office of Management and Budget were equally anxious to gather preliminary information on the impact of the reauthorization act before beginning the budgetary process. The committee felt that a round of interviews at an early date would capture information about the institutional and procedural changes taking place in the CETA system during the transition period. A preliminary report, issued in September 1979, summarized some of the highlights of the study from selected survey data.

The early timing of the survey imposed limitations on the study. In some cases, the respondents were not able to provide reliable data. For that reason, the number of respondents varies among the tables, and the findings drawn from tables with few respondents are qualified in the report. Caution must be exercised in generalizing from them. Despite these limitations, the committee believes that the report provides useful indications of changes in program direction and emerging problems.

ESTIMATING THE SIZE AND CHARACTERISTICS OF THE POPULATION ELIGIBLE FOR CETA PUBLIC SERVICE EMPLOYMENT PROGRAMS (PSE)

The estimates of the size and characteristics of the populations eligible for PSE under different eligibility requirements were derived from the Census Bureau's March 1978 Current Population Survey (CPS).[2] However, because the data collected in the CPS do not correspond precisely with the information needed to determine eligibility for PSE, some adjustments and assumptions were needed to arrive at the estimates in Table 13. These methodological considerations are outlined below.

AFDC RECIPIENTS

Both the 1976 and 1978 CETA amendments made AFDC recipients eligible for some PSE positions irrespective of their labor force status. In some cases, AFDC recipients were a substantial proportion of the eligible population. However, not all AFDC recipients are actually available for work. Thus, only AFDC recipients who were registered as available for work under the Work Incentive Program (WIN) were included in the eligible population estimates. To accomplish this, the CPS data were used to identify the non-AFDC eligible population. Cumulative data on the characteristics of WIN registrants for fiscal 1977 were then combined with the data on the non-AFDC group to obtain the profile of the total eligible population. This procedure also tends to correct for the undercount of AFDC recipients in the CPS.[3] The characteristics of AFDC and non-AFDC eligibles are shown separately in Table 13.

DURATION OF UNEMPLOYMENT

The eligibility requirements for PSE require a person to be unemployed for a certain number of weeks within a longer period of time, 15 out of 20 weeks for example. Due to the limitations imposed by the data collected in the CPS, the estimates shown in Table 13 are for the required period of unemployment (15 weeks for example) within a 52-week period. This will tend to overstate the size of the eligible population.

FAMILY INCOME

The PSE eligiblity requirements also specify the period of time over which family income will be annualized for purposes of determining eligibility—usually three or six months. The estimates in Table 14 are based on a family's annual income. Thus, a person in a family that had no income for three months but had significant earnings for the other nine months of the year would be excluded from the estimated eligible population even though at one point during the year that person would have met the family income requirement. This limitation on the estimates tends to understate the true size of the eligible population.

The income levels used to determine whether a person met the eligibility criteria (70 percent of the Bureau of Labor Statistics lower living standard, for example) were national averages that had not been adjusted for regional or farm/nonfarm differentials. Thus, a person in the CPS sample living in a geographic area with a low cost of living is more likely to be included in the estimated eligible population than a person in a high-cost area. It is not known how this affects the estimated size of the population.

In short, the estimates shown in Table 13 are approximations based on the data that are available. While not precise depictions of the true population eligible for CETA services, they do allow a comparison of the effects that different eligibility criteria have on the eligible population.

NOTES

1. Prime sponsors are city or county governments for jurisdictions of 100,000 or more population or consortia of several jurisdictions. State governments are sponsors for remaining units in the balance of state. The number of prime sponsors has been increased since the sample was drawn by subdivision of some large sponsors.

2. Unpublished tables prepared by the Bureau of Labor Statistics.

3. Unidentified AFDC recipients could be included in the non-AFDC CPS group. However, the problem of duplicate counts is likely to be minimal because most of the unidentified recipients would be out of the labor force and thus excluded from the CPS unemployed population.

Appendix C:
Sample Employability
Development Plan

EMPLOYABILITY PLAN

PLAN # _____

NAME
Mr.
Miss
Mrs. _____
     Last   *First*   *MI*

SOCIAL
SECURITY NO. _____

ADDRESS _____ PHONE _____

1. Background Information

   a. Education: List highest grade completed: _____
      High School or GED Graduate: Yes ____   No ____
      College Graduate: Yes ____   No ____   If yes, degree: _____
   b. Training: Programs Participated In:
      OJT ☐   BVR ☐   VO TECH ☐   JOB CORPS ☐   Other ☐
      Name school or college and list courses or training which prepared client for work:

      _____
      _____
      _____

   c. WORK HISTORY: Enter Most Recent Job First

Name of Employer	Job Title & Duties (Describe Job)
Address	Reason for Leaving:
Started Ended	Wage $
Name of Employer	Job Title & Duties (Describe Job)
Address	Reason for Leaving:
Started Ended	Wage $
Name of Employer	Job Title & Duties (Describe Job)
Address	Reason for Leaving:
Started Ended	Wage $

2. TEST SCORES:

   Typing: WPM
   Errors:

   DAT SUMMARY: _____
   _____
   _____
   _____
   _____

3. COUNSELOR'S ASSESSMENT

   a. Client's ability to express himself/herself _____
      _____
      _____

   b. Client's attitude during Assessment process _____
      _____
      _____

176

c. Client's educational needs _____

_____

d. Client's skill training needs and interests _____

_____

e. Client's work adjustment needs _____

_____

f. Client's counseling needs _____

_____

g. Client's appearance _____

_____

h. Client's interest and goals _____

_____

i. Client's strengths and weaknesses as related to job interest _____

_____

j. Is client Job Ready: Yes ____ No ____
k. Summary of client's employability _____

_____

_____

_____

_____

4. CLIENT JOB/TRAINING PREFERENCE:

1. Type of Job _____ DOT Code _____ (Primary)
2. Type of Job _____ DOT Code _____ (Secondary)

5. YOUR OPINION OF CLIENT'S APTITUDE FOR:

1. Primary Choice _____ Yes ____ No ____
   Client able to do job _____ Yes ____ No ____
   Client able to do job, but no labor market demand ____ Yes ____ No ____
   Client able to do job with necessary training ____ Yes ____ No ____
   Unrealistic job choice _____ Yes ____ No ____
2. Secondary Choice _____ Yes ____ No ____
   Client able to do job _____ Yes ____ No ____
   Client able to do job, but no labor market demand ____ Yes ____ No ____
   Client able to do job with necessary training ____ Yes ____ No ____
   Unrealistic job choice _____ Yes ____ No ____

6. ASSESSOR DETERMINED PLACEMENT OBJECTIVE:

Type of Job _____ DOT Code _____
Labor Market Demand: Very Good ____ Good ____ Fair ____
Job Qualifications necessary to placement objective _____

_____

177

7. TRAINING SERVICES	Hours/ Week	Starting Date	End Date Planned Actual	No. of Weeks to Complete Objective
a) Educational Objectives				
b) Skill Training Objectives				
c) Vocational Education Obj.				
d) Upgrading Objectives				
e) OJT: Job Title/Site				
f) Work Experience Objective				
g) Counseling Objectives				
h) Others				

8. SUPPORTIVE SERVICE NEEDS:

Child Care: _____

Medical: _____

Legal: _____

Housing: _____

Transportation: _____

OTHER COMMENTS:

Participant's Signature _____ Date _____
Counselor's Signature _____ Date _____

Appendix D:
Selected Legislative
Changes Under
CETA Reauthorization

PLANNING AND ADMINISTRATION

PLANS

Title I, Sect. 103, requires prime sponsors to submit a master plan that represents a long-term agreement between the sponsor and DOL, and an annual plan that describes in detail all programs that will be administered by the prime sponsor in the coming year. Previously, separate planning documents were required for each title.

PLANNING COUNCIL

Title I, Sect. 109, requires that the local planning council members represent a broader array of groups than previously designated, including significant segments of the eligible population, workers not represented by organized labor, veterans, handicapped individuals, vocational education agencies, public assistance agencies, and agricultural employers and workers. It also requires that comments and recommendations of the

Except where otherwise indicated, legislative references are to the Comprehensive Employment and Training Act Amendments of 1978, PL 95-524, October 27, 1978; and references to regulations are to the Department of Labor, Employment and Training Administration, Comprehensive Employment and Training Act Regulations, April 3, 1979.

private industry council (newly established under Title VII) be specifically considered. The chairperson of the local planning council must be chosen from the general public. The council must meet at least five times per year.

ADMINISTRATIVE EXPENDITURES

Title VI, Sect. 603, requires that no more than 10 percent of the funds allocated in fiscal 1979 under this title (countercyclical public service employment) be used for administrative purposes, and no more than 15 percent in any fiscal year thereafter. The previous limit was 15 percent.

Title IID, Sect. 232, requires that no more than 10 percent of the funds allocated under this title (public service employment for the economically disadvantaged) be used for administrative purposes. The previous limit was 15 percent.

Title I, Sect. 123(f), allows administrative funds to be commingled among titles. Previously, separate accounts were kept for each title.

REPORTING

Title I, Sect. 127(d), requires a new and detailed annual report that includes data on program performance, various cross-tabulations of participant characteristics, average cost per participant, and information about the postprogram experiences of participants.

OFFICE OF MANAGEMENT ASSISTANCE

Title I, Sect. 135, requires the secretary to establish an Office of Management Assistance to provide help to all prime sponsors who request or are identified as needing such services.

TARGETING PUBLIC SERVICE EMPLOYMENT PROGRAM PARTICIPANTS

ELIGIBILITY REQUIREMENTS FOR PUBLIC SERVICE EMPLOYMENT

Title IID, Sect. 236, requires that a Title IID participant be: (1) unemployed for at least 15 weeks and economically disadvantaged; or (2) a member of a family receiving Aid to Families with Dependent Children

(AFDC) or Supplemental Security Income (SSI). The term "economically disadvantaged" refers to a person who is a member either of a welfare family or of a family whose annual income is not in excess of (1) the Office of Management and Budget poverty level or (2) 70 percent of the lower living standard level. (The lower living standard level is determined on the basis of family budgets published by the Bureau of Labor Statistics.) Certain other persons, such as state-supported foster children and handicapped persons, are also included as economically disadvantaged.

Title VI, Sect. 607, requires that a Title VI participant be: (1) unemployed for at least 10 of the last 12 weeks and unemployed at the time of determination; and (2) an individual (a) whose family income does not exceed 100 percent of the lower living standard income level or (b) whose family receives AFDC or SSI.

Before the reauthorization act there were two rules that applied to Title VI eligibility: (1) A person hired for new positions (and half of the Title VI positions that became vacant through attrition) had to be (a) unemployed for at least 15 weeks and a member of a family whose income was below 70 percent of the lower living standard income level or (b) a member of a family receiving AFDC; (2) a person hired for the remaining Title VI positions that were vacant due to attrition was required only to have been unemployed for 30 days (15 days in areas with unemployment rates of 7 percent or more).

SPECIAL GROUPS

Title I, Sect. 122, provides that PSE is intended for the most severely disadvantaged in terms of length of unemployment and prospects for finding employment; that special consideration be given to persons receiving or eligible for public assistance and to disabled or Vietnam-era veterans; and that special emphasis be given to persons with particular labor market disadvantages, including offenders, persons with limited English proficiency, handicapped individuals, women, single parents, displaced homemakers, youth, older workers, and individuals who lack education credentials. This considerably expands the groups receiving particular consideration or emphasis in PSE programs, and de-emphasizes unemployment insurance beneficiaries and exhaustees who were previously among the target groups.

Title VI, Sect. 603(b), provides that special consideration be given to unemployed persons who have previous teaching experience and who are certified by the prime sponsor's state for filling teaching positions in elementary and secondary schools. No requirement of this type was included in the previous CETA legislation.

PSE SERVICES AND JOBS

PSE FOR THE STRUCTURALLY UNEMPLOYED

Before the reauthorization act, Title II authorized a PSE program in areas with at least 6.5 percent unemployment. The reauthorization act established a PSE program (Title IID) for the structurally unemployed, regardless of the area unemployment rate.

Countercyclical PSE remains under Title VI. The program is activated only when the national rate of unemployment is above 4 percent, and is designed to expand and contract corresponding to changes in the unemployment rate.

WAGES

Title I, Sect. 122(i), establishes a maximum annual PSE wage of $10,000 except in high-wage areas, where a maximum of up to $12,000 may be established based on an area wage index published by the secretary.

Title I, Sect. 122(i), establishes a national annual average PSE wage equivalent to $7,200. This lowers the national average annual PSE wage by $600. Local average rates must be adjusted according to an area wage index published by the secretary. The index is based on the relationship of wages in each area to a national average.

WAGE SUPPLEMENTATION

Title IID, Sect. 237, forbids supplementation of CETA PSE wages from local funds for Title IID participants, except for persons receiving such supplementation on September 30, 1978. Wage supplementation was permitted under the previous legislation.

Title VI, Sect. 609, allows wage supplementation up to 10 percent of the maximum allowable wage in the area for Title VI PSE participants.

Supplementation may be as much as 20 percent in areas with an annual average wage in employment covered by unemployment insurance between 125 percent and 150 percent of the national average wage in such employment. Wage supplementation was not previously limited under Title VI.

PROJECTS

Title VI, Sect. 605(a), provides that 50 percent of Title VI funds be used for short-duration projects. Under the Emergency Jobs Programs Extension Act of 1976 (EJPEA) all new positions were to be in projects. Projects are defined as tasks that can be accomplished in a definite time period, result in a specific product, and would not be done with existing funds.

DURATION OF PROJECTS

Title VI, Sect. 605, limits the duration of projects to 18 months, but allows them to be renewed for another 18 months, provided that they are successful in meeting the purposes of the act. Previously, a project was limited to a 12-month duration.

USE OF NONPROFIT AGENCIES

DOL regulations require that at least one-third of Title VI project funds be allotted to nonprofit organizations. Prior to the reauthorization the conference report accompanying the Emergency Jobs Programs Extension Act of 1976 (which amended CETA) urged prime sponsors to provide project positions to nonprofit organizations, but the regulations did not specify a goal.

DURATION OF PARTICIPATION

Title I, Sect. 122, limits participation in PSE to 78 weeks in a five-year period. (Under the act, not more than 26 weeks of enrollment prior to October 1978 can be counted for this purpose.) Waivers of the 78-week limit may be granted in cases of unusual hardship. Tenure was not limited before reauthorization.

TRANSITION TO UNSUBSIDIZED EMPLOYMENT

EMPLOYABILITY DEVELOPMENT PLANS

Title II, Sect. 205, requires prime sponsors to establish a personalized employability plan for each Title IID participant, and to review and assess that plan periodically. These plans were not previously required.

TRAINING AND SUPPORT SERVICES

Title IID, Sect. 232(b)(2), requires that at least 10 percent of fiscal 1979 Title IID PSE funds, 15 percent of 1980 funds, 20 percent of 1981 funds, and 22 percent of 1982 funds be used exclusively for training.

Title VI, Sect. 603(a), and Sect. 605(c) require that at least 10 percent of

Title VI PSE funds for fiscal 1979 and 5 percent of such funds in all subsequent years be used for training and employability counseling and services for those participants who, based on an assessment of employability, require these services.

MONITORING AND ELIGIBILITY VERIFICATION

MONITORING

Title I, Sect. 121(q), and Sect. 676.61 of the regulations require that prime sponsors establish independent monitoring units and require that subrecipients establish independent monitoring units when feasible. Sect. 123(g) of the act and Sect. 676 of the regulations set forth the specific problems that were of greatest concern to Congress. These problems include kickbacks, commingling of funds, charging of fees, nepotism, child labor, political patronage, political activities, lobbying activities, sectarian activities, unionization and antiunionization activities, maintenance of effort, theft or embezzlement, improper inducement, and obstruction of investigations.

ELIGIBILITY VERIFICATION

Pursuant to Sect. 123(i) of the act, Sect. 676.75-3 of the regulations provides specific instructions for eligibility verification, which include (1) obtaining a completed application, signed by the applicant, (2) a desk review of each application for consistency and reasonableness within 30 days of the date of enrollment, and (3) verification and documentation of a quarterly sample (not to exceed 10 percent) of the enrollees for the preceding three months. Previous regulations did not stipulate specific verification procedures.

LIABILITY PROVISIONS

Sect. 123(i) and Sect. 106(d) of the act provide that the prime sponsor be held financially liable for ineligible participants who were enrolled deliberately or with insufficient care. Sect. 676.75-3 of the DOL regulations holds prime sponsors financially liable, but provides that reponsibility for eligibility determination may be delegated with provisions for transferring liability to the delegatee. In cases where funds cannot be recovered from that party the prime sponsor remains liable. Previous regulations held no one liable if eligibility determination was performed by the employment service. Sect. 106(1) of the act provides that any person

*2284-14
1982
5-12
C

who alleges that an action of a prime sponsor violates any provisions of the act or the regulations may pursue any remedies authorized under federal, state, or local law. Sect. 676.74 of the regulations specifies that 18 U.S.C. 665 provides criminal penalties for knowingly hiring ineligible individuals under the act.